IN
THEIR
OWN
WAY

IN

ACCEPTING YOUR

THEIR

CHILDREN FOR

OWN

WHO THEY ARE

WAY

Karen Johnson Zurheide
Jeffry R. Zurheide

Augsburg
MINNEAPOLIS

IN THEIR OWN WAY
Accepting Your Children for Who They Are

Scripture quotations are from the New Revised Standard Version Bible, copyright © 1989 by the Division of Christian Education of the National Council of the Churches of Christ in the U.S.A. and used by permission.

Cover design by David Meyer
Book design by Timothy W. Larson

Library of Congress Cataloging-in-Publication Data

Zurheide, Karen Johnson.
  In their own way: accepting your children for who they are / Karen Johnson, Jeffry Zurheide.
    p. cm.
  Includes bibliographical references.
  ISBN 0-8066-3957-1 (alk. paper)
  1. Parenting—Religious aspects—Christianity. 2. Problem children—Religious life. 3.Handicapped children—Religious life. I. Zurheide, Jeffry R., 1955– II. Title.

BV4529.Z87 2000
248.8'45—dc21   00-035468

The paper used in this publication meets the minimum requirements of American National Standard for Information Sciences—Permanence of Paper for Printed Library Materials, ANSI Z329.48-1984.

Manufactured in the U.S.A.   AF 9-3957

04   03   02   01   00   1   2   3   4   5   6   7   8   9   10

To Molly and Andrew—
We could never stop loving you!

Contents

It is only natural that as parents our hopes and expectations for our children are high. Regardless of how we may define it, we want "the best" for them. Often, however, our hopes for our children must go unmet. There can be any number of causes for such parental disappointment. Our purpose here is not to discuss those causes specifically but to help readers recognize that whenever real life shatters our expectations, we hurt. We need grace.

Our feelings as parents are always powerful. This is especially true when we are unable to control or positively influence our children's circumstances. We may respond to the loss of our dreams for them with intense feelings of sadness, embarrassment, anger, and responsibility. These feelings, left unaddressed, can lead to grief, seclusion, bitterness, and guilt. Added to these, nearly all hurting parents share feelings of isolation. It is possible, however, to heal some of these great hurts, and there are ways to move out of isolation.

Popular Christianity leads us to expect blessing for a life of faith. The biblical message, however, tells us that God does not mete out rewards and punishments for our works. Rather, God understands our suffering and is present with us in it. With God's grace, then, we can live out the parental responsibilities of faithfulness, love, and forgiveness.

As God accepts us and we receive God's grace, we learn to accept our children as they are. We can even find ways to embrace their uniqueness. When we begin to relinquish our earlier dreams and replace them with new, and hopefully more realistic, ones, we offer our children grace. In this process, we are less defined by our children and their struggles, even as we become vulnerable to the lessons we learn from them.

Introduction
The "Perfect" Child

How many hopes and fears, how many ardent wishes and anxious apprehensions are twisted together in the threads that connect the parent with the child!

—Samuel G. Goodrich

ALTHOUGH OUR OWN CHILDREN are hardly old enough to be the sole sources on which to base this book, for decades we have observed the struggles and disappointments—small and great—of those with adolescent or grown children. We have watched our parents and their peers suffer along with their children. We have seen our own friends ache when their children chose poorly. As a pastor, Jeff has counseled with parents hurting deeply over their children for any number of reasons. While director of a statewide parent support network, Karen often heard parents of children with birth defects lament the medically based limitations that threatened their children's futures. Clearly, the effect on parents of their children's imperfections and failures can be, in one way or another, monumental.

We wish we could make it all better for you and your children. We wish we could offer solutions for fixing your children's problems. While many books do offer techniques and strategies to assist parents in helping their children, that is not the purpose of this book. Instead, we offer parents a way to live on in the midst of it all, whether or not things get better for their children. We offer parents God's grace.

EXPECTATIONS

Even before we become parents, an entire mountain of expectations for our children is beginning to take shape. Parenting overflows with hopeful anticipation from its very outset, with a precious baby being a bundle of pure potential. If healthy at birth, our new children seem to have limitless potential.

Like countless generations of parents before us, we modern mothers and fathers want nothing but "the best" for our children. Some of our expectations for them, such as good health, are instinctive. Others are more personal, perhaps relating to what we ourselves have accomplished—or failed to achieve. Some expectations, such as a higher education, may be the result of societal norms. Still others are prompted by advertising that relentlessly teases us with pictures of the American good life—beauty, success, fame, fortune. Yes, that is what we want for our children. We want it all.

These expectations for children may be conscious—clear to us, even obvious to those around us. Or they may be so deeply ingrained that, as long as they are easily met, we are not explicitly aware of them.

Stop for a moment. Think about the early expectations you had for your child. To start with, you anticipated a healthy baby. You would do your best to assure your growing child's well-being so that he or she would develop on a normal timetable into a strong, physically fit youth and adult. Should there be any health concerns along the way, God forbid, modern medicine would resolve them.

Your desire for your child's good health and safekeeping was natural parental protectiveness at work, observable throughout the animal kingdom. But avoidance of deadly disease and accident is not what every human parent has always expected. In times past, infant and child mortality rates were extremely high. Life was less safe, and life expectancies were short. This is true even today in many parts of the world. But in the United States and other developed nations, we generally assume our children will live long and survive us by at least a couple decades.

Beyond good health, you no doubt anticipated that your child would be bright and inquisitive, a child who would catch on quickly and do reasonably well in school. You thought you would encourage your child's cognitive development by reading together, discussing school experiences, helping with homework, and fostering learning in every form. You were certain your child would at least match your intelligence and your own level of educational accomplishment.

As to appearances, you expected your child to look beautiful, handsome—resembling you, only better! If necessary, you would find a way to pay for the braces or the diet camp or whatever else it might take to maximize your child's attractive appearance.

You further assumed, as any parent would, a well-adjusted, responsible, hard-working child, who would make wise occupational choices along life's way. Careers would be personally satisfying and monetarily rewarding. Your child would be financially independent, even successful. It surely would be an added bonus if that child could support you in your old age!

Not to overlook what really matters, you also expected a loving, grateful child, with whom you would be emotionally close. You two would nearly always get along, with the normal exceptions of toddlerhood struggles and adolescent rebellion, neither of which would be of great consequence.

More specifically, your expectations may even have included a child who would share your particular talents and interests. Imagine how wonderful it would be to enjoy together music or sports or movies. And even more wonderful, to be bound together by common values and a mutually vital faith in God.

Such closeness to you would be mirrored in the well-chosen, deep friendships your child would make and in a loving, compatible marriage. Eventually, the happy couple would go on to have nearly perfect children—your grandchildren!—making yet another perfect family. All in all, your nearly perfect child, with a minor rough edge or two just to make life interesting, would bring you great joy and make you proud.

While perhaps no one really thinks his or her child's life will be so completely without problems, our hopes and dreams are surely for our children's lives to be trouble-free. And, at the beginning, before real life gets in the way, this is what we innocently expect.

In today's child-centered culture, parents are under greater pressure than ever to produce perfect children. After all, we present-day parents are far more enlightened than the generations preceding us. We know the psychology behind raising children. We have learned about facilitating communication and promoting self-esteem. We understand the importance of quality time. Being more educated and sophisticated, there is a greater likelihood that we will raise children who are successful and contribute positively to society. At least that is what we are led to believe.

It was five years ago, on a Connecticut playground, that Karen shared a fascinating conversation about family size with a mother of two young daughters. The other woman said she and her husband had been considering having a third child. They were uncertain. But they reasoned that this was something they could contribute to the world. Another child of theirs.

Karen was flabbergasted. She bit her tongue and strained to disguise her disbelief. For she had never thought of children of particular parents as being gifts-in-advance to the world. It seemed audacious to assume that one's children were guaranteed to be something special from whom the world could benefit. Just why should that be the case?

Why would the child of educated, well-to-do, "good" people be or do any more for this world of ours than a child of the slums of Calcutta? Who could know? Does the world really need another investment banker who lives in a tidy suburb, for instance? Would this particular child give back more to the world than the resources that he or she would consume? And even if from a "good" home, how could a mother be so sure her child would turn out well? This was a confident expectation, to say the least.

While perhaps not assuming our children would be gifts to the world, we have had our share of expectations for each of our children. In addition to instinctive expectations, we two came at parenting with thirty-plus years each of accumulated societal expectations. Added to that, we were inundated with expectation-creating baby literature and advertisements while Karen was pregnant with our first child.

We are still not sure how those advertisers uncovered us. But find us they did, as evidenced by ever-mounting piles of baby catalogs, whose purpose was to convince us to purchase every possible gizmo and gadget to assure the health and comfort of our little tyke. How happy those adorable babies and toddlers were in the ads! That is what our kid would be like if we did a good job of parenting—and purchasing. Or so we naïvely thought.

REALITY

It is a testimony to human optimism—or naïveté—that we assume until proven otherwise that our parenting dreams will be fulfilled. Aside from the threat of first-trimester miscarriage and the anxious moments of routine prenatal testing, we pretty much take for granted that all will be well.

With our first child we were introduced, five weeks before our baby's due date, to the harsh truth that expectations of parents do not always match reality. If not a perfect experience, we had expected pregnancy and childbirth to proceed normally. We had no reason to think otherwise. We were both healthy. Karen had done all the "right" things during her pregnancy, being careful about diet, exercise, and rest, avoiding exposure to substances in food, drink, or the environment that could be harmful to our baby. None of our known relatives had ever given birth to other than a perfect baby.

Yet our tiny girl, delivered by emergency cesarean section, was far from perfect. We discovered that she suffered from a rare genetic anomaly that affected every cell of her frail body. The future was a blur, as our dreams for our child vanished before they could fully take shape. All our hopes for her were quickly dashed when our precious firstborn died twenty-four hours after birth.

We would never reduce our child's life to a mere lesson. Never. But she did teach us, against our will, that parental control of children's health and physical well-being is severely limited.

This was a difficult lesson for us young, middle-class American parents, who, up to that point, had been pretty well able to control our lives. It was a lesson with which most parents are not confronted so soon. As long as all is well, we parents think that we are in control, that we are keeping our children safe and healthy. But this perception changes when we come up against something bigger than we are.

Years after losing our first child, Karen directed a statewide support network for parents of young children in medical crisis. The early parenting experiences of this group included prematurity and its complications, congenital defects, genetic syndromes, and developmental delays. Like us, this unfortunate group of parents had been shocked with an unwanted, difficult lesson: Despite their best efforts, parents cannot always control their children's health. In some cases, it is impossible.

Through their offspring, these parents learned more than they ever cared to about life-saving medications, complicated surgical procedures, medical research and technology, and physical and occupational therapies. While they could learn about all of this and have some control in their children's treatment, they could not truly control the course that their children would take or the ultimate outcome.

Beyond medical expertise, parents in the group learned about lost dreams and dashed expectations. Whether their children's conditions were temporary or permanent, these parents struggled emotionally. When the struggle was not with death, it was largely with the fact that their children were not perfect and that countless normal and reasonable expectations for those children promised to go unfulfilled.

In spite of our own initial loss as parents, we had hope enough to expect a subsequent "successful" pregnancy. That hope was tested by an early miscarriage before we welcomed our second baby, a healthy daughter—bald as an egg, but so beautiful to us. (Hair was never an expectation, as Karen spent her own first year or two with the same hairless-do.) Off to such a good start, we had planned out—at least on some subconscious level—a perfect future for our girl. Within weeks of her birth, however, there were hints that our daughter would challenge our expectations. Thankfully, she remained healthy and developed normally. But it was not just her body that was strong. Our tiny girl had ideas of her own. And through her, we encountered yet another harsh reality: Parents have no control over the personalities of their children.

Our children are who they are, from the very start. This conclusion is not based on scientific research, but on facts infinitely more persuasive and more compelling than studies and statistics could ever be. Our conclusion comes from personal experience, the observation of our children and countless others, as well as passionate reporting from nearly every parent we know.

One of the first clues our daughter gave us of her individuality concerned physical closeness. To most people, a word that just naturally goes along with *baby* is *cuddle*. Cuddling is what you want to do with a precious little one. And that is usually what they enjoy as well. And cuddling is what we assumed we would spend a good bit of time doing with our baby.

But not our girl. She wanted none of it. Oh, she liked attention—to be held, to be bounced and walked around—almost constantly. But she did not like people in her face. She was not going to play that coochy-coochy game. Not this kid! In a telling early photograph, she can be seen straining to turn away from her cuddling mother. We had to wonder. What kind of child would recoil from her parent? What kind of mother would cause a child to recoil? Where did this response come from? Where would it lead?

Our child's unwillingness to cuddle is but a small example of innate personality traits, but the truth it illustrates is significant. With a sick and dying first baby, we had already learned the hard way that we could not control the health of our offspring. Now we also were seeing that we could not control personality, general disposition, or innate preferences. This child would not be a lovey-dovey cuddler, and there was nothing we could do about it.

We, however, were slow to accept this new wisdom. We reasoned that as time went on, in spite of any seemingly negative personality traits, we ought to be able to shape this child's behavior. By using techniques recommended by the experts—as outlined in any number of parenting books—we would surely, for instance, be able to make our standoffish child more sociable. We would help her, with loving example and appropriate discipline, to modify her behavior. We would pray for her and for ourselves. It might take a while, but with diligence we would succeed in our effort.

Well, maybe. And maybe not. For our little girl had a will of her own. Make that a very strong will. We would soon discover that our true control of her behavior, even in the early years, would be minimal. We would see that it was more likely that she would shape us than the other way around.

As it turns out, our child was not so unusual. She may have been more intense and less compliant than the average child, but children—

from a very early age—make their own choices, choices that parents cannot truly control. We can model, teach, guide, provide boundaries, and discipline. But we cannot live our children's lives for them. We have modest control of our young children's actions during their childhood and virtually no control in their adult lives.

While our daughter and her younger brother have their unique personalities, with both positive and negative aspects, things have gone fairly smoothly for them so far. Our disappointments over them and for them have been relatively minor.

But who knows what will befall our children in the future? Who knows how their personalities, for better or for worse, will unfold? Who knows what choices they will make, especially important decisions? What will be their misfortunes, their mistakes, and their intentional misbehaviors? And what will be the consequences?

One thing is certain. Between the bad things that will happen to them and the mistakes they will make, our children will not be the perfect beings living the perfect lives that we had once imagined. This is not pessimism. This is reality. For many parents it is a very harsh reality.

Do not be fooled. Regardless of what those glowing Christmas newsletters report, any honest parent will tell you that there is no such thing as a perfect child! We have yet to receive a Christmas letter that reads, "Elizabeth is in rehab; Will is flunking out of college; and Cindi has slept with every man in town." Real life is frequently not the stuff of happy greetings.

While each parent has different ideals for each child, it is certainly true that no child ever totally measures up to any parent's expectations. The list of what parents may honestly consider to be "imperfections" in children goes on and on. Such imperfections may be innocently visited upon our children or brought on by themselves, intentionally or accidentally. And these imperfections may be more troublesome for parents than children. Here is a sampling of challenges, in a wide range of severity, that parents may experience in their children:

- addictions or substance abuse
- career or job struggle or failure
- criminal activity and incarceration

- disease
- eating disorders
- educational struggle or failure
- emotional disorders
- financial difficulties
- marital struggle or failure
- physical or mental disabilities
- poor parenting of their children
- rejection of faith, church, values
- suicide
- "unacceptable" sexual behavior
- underachievement—in many forms

Accompanying any of these problems, we may encounter the even greater challenge of estrangement from our children, perhaps the most difficult and disappointing life experience for parents. More than anything else, we parents want to be emotionally close to our children. Ongoing emotional separation from them causes profound pain.

If the problem that you believe your child is facing is not on the above list, this book is still for you. For this book is not about resolving children's particular problems. This book is meant, rather, to help parents personally cope with their children's problems and the difficulties they present.

RESULT

There is no precise formula to predict how a particular parent will respond to a particular problem with a particular child. The parent, the child, and the problem are individually unique variables. Combine them all and you have a situation that cannot be duplicated.

Some of the circumstances parents encounter in their children can be adapted to more easily than others. And some parents are better able to adjust their expectations when necessary. This capability may be a matter of personality, of natural flexibility. It may indicate a more accepting attitude, a higher tolerance for change, a clearer grasp of reality.

Most parents do set high goals for their children, wanting the very best for them. But, with this attitude comes a high potential for disappointment. Consequently, there is less chance for their expectations to go unfulfilled. Setting lower goals would be one way to protect ourselves, to minimize the chances of unfulfilled expectations. If, for example, a set of parents assumes that their child will marry poorly, struggle through a loveless marriage, and go through a bitter divorce, anything less awful than this scenario occurring in their child's love relationships will be good news. But intentionally setting unrealistically low expectations of our children cheats them and us. It is no real solution.

The bottom line is that most parents, given enough time, will have a fair share of their expectations for their children go unmet. This means there will be painful disappointments. And some parents will experience more than their fair share, becoming all too acquainted with the kind of gut-wrenching pain that plagues them over time and cries out for mercy—from God, from others, and even from their condemning selves.

When children experience difficulties, parents often experience the painful frustration of helpless love. Parents would like the ability to change the present for their children—not to mention the past and future—into something more positive, more productive, more whole, more satisfying. But the reach of parental influence, even when armed with money or other powerful resources, can be awfully short.

One of the chief tenets of the Al-Anon organization, which offers support for families of alcoholics, is that we are not, ultimately, responsible for the actions of others, even those we love dearly. Applied to parenting, this principle affirms the reality that we cannot truly control our children's actions or force positive change on them. This is a hard truth, but it is one that encourages us to focus on being responsible for what we can control—namely, our own attitudes and actions.

Consider Expectations and Reality

1. Name some expectations you had for your child long ago.
2. What has disappointed you about your child?
3. How serious are these "failures" of your child?
4. Name some more recent expectations you have had for your child.
5. What is the current status of your relationship with your child?

—1—

The Need for Grace

"Blessed are those who mourn, for they will be comforted."

—Matthew 5:4

WHILE SUFFERING PARENTS MIGHT CHOOSE, for various understandable reasons, to push down their pain and the problems that give rise to it, it is hard to find healing for undisclosed wounds. We begin here, therefore, by illuminating the pain parents can reasonably expect. In shining a bright spotlight on parental anguish, our purpose is not to inflict more pain but to bring parental hurt into the light in preparation for healing. As you allow the truth of your anguish to be illuminated, you will move toward the place where you can find comfort.

POWERFUL PARENTAL FEELINGS

From the confirmation of a pregnancy or the call from the adoption agency through the rest of our lives, we parents are powerfully attached to our children. Before we had children, our own parents would tell us, "Just wait until you have kids. Then you will understand." They were right. It is only then that we can really understand what it is to feel so entirely responsible for another life, so totally bound up in the welfare of someone else, so committed to the well-being of a child.

From the very beginning, parental instinct, whether maternal or paternal, works overtime in us to nurture and protect. That is particularly true when our children are young and physically vulnerable, when they so clearly need us just to survive. But, as the saying goes, Once a parent, always a parent.

And the same is true of our parents. In fact, we chuckle when our own parents still worry about such everyday things as our safety when we travel. Sometimes, to save them undue concern, it seems preferable not to let them know that we are on the road or in the air. They will not worry, we reason, about what they do not know.

No matter their age, our parents' concern for us continues, encompassing the decisions we make, both large and small. One of our parents not long ago refused to buy Jeff a requested ax for Christmas to be used for cutting firewood. They thought he might hurt himself. A newly divorced friend reported how her mother worried about her when she had a cold with "no one to take care of her." While practical and legal responsibility may end when a child reaches adulthood, parental desire for a child to be happy, healthy, and successful never ends.

Beyond the seemingly hardwired sense of physical responsibility and care, we mothers and fathers are naturally full of emotion when it comes to our children. All of our feelings—including love, fear, and anger—are intensified when they have to do with our children. Our children call forth from us the very deepest of feelings—the greatest love, the most overwhelming joy, the most terrifying fear, the darkest sadness, even tremendous anger. More than anyone else, they can—and do!—bring to us the highest highs and the lowest lows. This too is instinct, this is commitment, this is a closeness that no other relationship can duplicate.

Similarly, our parental emotions run strong when it comes to problems our children have, whether they bring them on themselves or not. We want to shield our children from trouble, we want to make good choices for them, we want to defend them when they are wronged. With our desire to see things turn out well for our children, it is nearly impossible for a parent to let go. Yet letting go does need to happen for both parent and child. And it needs to happen not overnight, but step-by-step along life's way.

As much as we may want things to be otherwise, in this imperfect world of ours it is inevitable that our children will experience pain. And that pain will be of a physical nature, to be sure. But more significantly, our children will experience emotional hurts. In her book *Learning with Molly,* Karen writes of her experience with our second daughter: "Many parents try to shelter their beloved offspring from hurt of any kind. Given pain's inevitability, perhaps less parental energy should be expended avoiding hardship for children, and more devoted to teaching how to face pain and survive its hurt."

Parents ache on behalf of their hurting children. But sometimes we parents worry and hurt for our children when they seem not to worry or hurt. For instance, a child who chooses to be a beach bum may be very happy. At the same time, his or her parents may be going crazy with worry, disappointment, and disapproval over the child's choice. There are many choices our children can make that seem fine to them but are troublesome to us, their parents. Our standards, our expectations, are not always those of our children.

It may not be admirable, but some parental pain actually seems to be selfish, more for us ourselves than for our children. But when deep-seated parental expectations are not met, even if there is no apparent, recognizable suffering by the child, parental disappointment hurts.

Self-centered disappointment can come from wanting to clone our own lives. We all know people who excelled in a certain realm and want nothing more than for a son or daughter to do the same, whether that means taking over the family business or succeeding in a sport, an art, an educational pursuit. The coach may want another athlete in the family. The dancer may want a child who possesses rhythm and grace. Or we may want our children to duplicate the kind of family lives we have known—married with children, for instance—whether or not that is what they want or are able to achieve.

In contrast, we may want our children to accomplish something we did not. We may think, "I dropped out of high school. It's always been my dream that my child would get the education that I missed." Or, "I should have gone further in sports, but my parents didn't support me in that. I'm going to do everything I can to see that my child accomplishes what I could not." Never mind what the child wants.

Other disappointment is not directly based on what has or has not happened in our own lives. But it is likewise a result of sincerely, though with a desire to control, "wanting the best" for our offspring. With the crystal ball of parental knowledge and experience, we are certain. Shouldn't the best include athleticism, popularity, college degree, "big" job, spouse, and children? Maybe for us. Maybe not for our children.

A flaw with all such thinking is the assumption that we omnisciently know what the "best" should look like. We can have it all planned out in our minds. But this plan is in our minds, not our children's. Although flawed, this brand of specific, personal parental disappointment is powerfully real. And we are easily seduced into thinking it is for our children, when it is actually for us and our own unfulfilled expectations.

Thinking back, much of our hurting those many years ago when we lost our first baby was self-pity. Our pain was more than suffering for our child who died peacefully, knowing nothing of the life she had missed. We wanted to be parents. We wanted a healthy child. We felt sorry for ourselves. Some parental pain is like that, with the loss being much more that of the parent than that of the child.

But most parental pain does involve suffering because one's child is suffering. If we are going to be honest, it is probably a mix of vicarious suffering for our child and suffering for ourselves. For when children hurt, parents hurt. We cannot help it. That is just what parents do.

To feel pain on behalf of one's child, even to suffer, for any of a vast array of reasons, is natural. Usually the depth of that pain in some way matches the objective significance of the problem. Given a list of failures in children, such as the one found in this book's introduction, we could rank each item according to its severity. Our orderings would differ somewhat, but they would probably match fairly closely. From an objective perspective, for example, which would be worse, that your child broke up with a potentially wonderful mate or that your child murdered a convenience store clerk? Obviously, the latter is worse.

Experientially, however, we are not provided with a list of potential problems that we can compare and objectively organize. In parenting, our experience is relative and subjective. If, for example, the worst trauma we have known with a child is his or her difficult break up, that turn of events can seem absolutely awful. Intellectually, we may be able to objectify the situation by comparing it to a more severe situation, hypothetical or real, outside of our experience. Emotionally, however, we subjectively feel the pain.

Karen, for example, once worked with a mother whose child had undergone more than twenty surgeries in the first eight years of life to correct multiple birth defects. Imagine how that family had been dealing over months and years with concern for that child's situation. Karen's coworker related that only recently had her child begun to successfully eat solid food and be weaned from a daily food pump. The child still required nightly enemas for bowel control. The family dealt with all this and more each day for many years.

What was really bothering this mother, though, was not something as difficult as her daughter's physical challenges. These had been faced from the beginning. Her pressing concern was that this otherwise bright child was struggling in math. You see, both parents had excelled in the subject. Working with numbers was easy for them and for their older child. They assumed it would be for this child, too. It was a big disappointment when she required math tutoring.

Even for these parents who knew firsthand the concerns of physical limitations, this minor learning problem was genuinely troublesome. Their daughter's difficulty with math did not fit their expectations; it did not match their dreams. It was a real disappointment.

We can learn from these parents. Experiencing subjective pain is human. We needn't minimize our own disappointments. While it can be helpful to put our disappointments in perspective, they are all valid and in need of healing. Even if your child's problem is objectively less serious than others, the pain and suffering you experience is still valid. Your need for healing is still real.

What's more, all parents have different personalities and different levels of tolerance for uncertainty and emotional pain. Some of us are natural worriers, making much out of little. Others of us walk through crises as if everything is totally normal, quietly handling them. Still others of us live in denial.

A problem that may seem minor to a parent whose child has been through much worse still has its own valid pain for the parent walking through that objectively lesser trauma. Yes, being sleep deprived because of a teenager who is out past curfew again is worse than being up with an inconsolable toddler. Yes, an adult child out of work is of greater concern than the preschooler who cannot stick to a task. But we parents must allow ourselves to hurt when it hurts, even if there are worse problems out there.

Regardless of the source and severity of our children's problems, we parents often hurt. We often hurt deeply. That is a fact. And if we are facing terrible times with our children, perhaps we can find some comfort in the fact that other parents are hurting, too.

PARENTAL RESPONSES

How do the harsh realities of children's problems make parents feel? What is the nature of parental pain? What shape does it take? Parents experience a broad range of feelings, based partly on the relative magnitude of their struggles. Parents may feel disappointed, discouraged, demoralized, devastated, numb. Parents may experience any or all of these feelings in response to their children's difficulties.

For parents, there are myriad responses to imperfection in children. In considering parental responses, we need to remember uniqueness. This applies to anything to do with people. And although situations and responses may be similar, they are never precisely the same. In Karen's work supporting parents of children with medical problems, for example, each family handled its crisis uniquely, even when children's medical experiences were very much alike.

Despite the uniqueness of their children's problems and their responses to them, parents hurting over their children do seem to share two experiences. They feel a lack of control and a loss of dreams.

Lack of Control

The parents Karen worked with had naturally expected to take healthy babies home soon after birth, to successfully care for their children, to be able to nurture and protect their little ones. Parents expected that they and their children would be like other families, reaching normal developmental milestones, such as chewing, talking, and taking first steps. But medical realities prevented the anticipated fulfillment of these expectations.

Failing to meet even those most basic, simple expectations gave parents a distinct feeling of being out of control. They were supposed to be the moms and dads, the ones who would care for and protect their children. But they could not do it, as the most basic elements of normal parenting were barred to them. They were supposed to have been in charge. Instead, they found themselves without much control in their children's lives.

Parents of older children can also feel this way. It is particularly noticeable when adolescents are stretching their wings or rebelling against parental authority. While there are usually family rules and expectations for behavior, parental control is minimal. Children, ultimately, think for themselves; they act independently; they make mistakes; they get in trouble; they feel their own pain.

When our children become adults and are living "on their own," we do not much expect to control them. But we would still like to think that we have an influence on them, that our input and opinions, our loving wisdom, might count for something. We would still like to be able to fix our children's problems, to make spouses and employers love them. But, truthfully, there is usually little we can do.

Loss of a Dream

The same parents with whom Karen worked had dreams, some spoken, others assumed, for their sons and their daughters. They had fully expected a bright, positive future for their children. But they were forced—sometimes in a moment, sometimes over a period of months or years—out of their positive expectations. Their dreams for their children would never become reality, remaining only as a source of pain.

For these parents, being robbed of their powerful, positive dreams was a loss that led to grief for an imagined, expected child. Adjusting their expectations, developing different dreams for the children they actually had—with their difficult deficits—would take time as they worked through their grief and the uncertainties of the future.

We can relate to lost dreams, as we have experienced this kind of parental pain. Our dreams for our first child never included her premature death. But that is what happened. We were forced to give up our dreams for that baby and cope with our loss.

But situations in our children's lives do not have to be as severe as illness or death for parents to experience the pain of the loss of dreams. Reviewing expectations for our two other children's futures, for example, our dreams definitely *do not* include hearing an unmarried teenage daughter confess that she is pregnant, learning that a grown son is rejecting wife and children in favor of career, discovering that a child is an alcoholic who refuses treatment, or dozens of other troubling scenarios. Like the parents who lost their dreams for their newborn children, such news would steal our dreams and leave us with uncertainty for our children's futures.

If you are a parent of a child who in one significant way or another has shattered your expectations, you may also have felt lack of control and the loss of a dream. The emotions that stem from such loss are many. The following sections address some of these common parental feelings, which may occur alone, or, as is more likely, in combination. Perhaps some of these are familiar to you.

Sadness

Though not a very powerful word, sadness describes a gnawing, nagging feeling of hurt. Many parents carry sadness with them on a daily basis. They are sad that their child will not reach the potential seen in him or her, sad that health or intellect is being wasted, sad that their child is hurting, sad that their child hurt another person, sad for any number of reasons.

Feelings of sadness may come and go. They may be temporarily forgotten during distracting happy experiences. But we have seen many cases in which sadness pervades most of a parent's day-to-day living.

Fuel for parental sadness is often found in the strained parent-child relationship that can accompany children's problems. If communication is poor or broken, the sense of sadness can grow. If children disregard their parents' opinions or feelings, if they shut parents out of their lives, sadness can darken parents' days.

Embarrassment and Shame

Although they are distinctly their own people, society often views children as extensions of their parents. Truthfully, it is hard not to feel as if they represent us in some way to the world. Parents love to feel the swell of pride, privately and often publicly, when their children succeed or do something well: "That's my child, you know," we think or say. "Yes, that one, who...." And we mean the one who received the honor, who has the terrific spouse, who was praised in the newspaper, and so on. Conversely, we feel ashamed or embarrassed when our children fail, especially with society's high expectations of accomplishment and success.

But are children's actions, accomplishments, and failures really reliable reflections of their parents? For instance, with our two children, who will seldom look an adult in the eye and answer clearly, their public behavior often does not reflect the fact that we are teaching them the same manners and social skills as other parents whose children impress with their social grace. We can encourage our kids, with both positive and negative reinforcement, to behave as we would like. But we cannot force them.

Realistic expectations are important. Parents cannot actually change their children's personalities or innate abilities, forcing the shy child to be suddenly outgoing or the tone-deaf child musical. A different personality might make for a better public impression, reflecting more positively on parents. It might save us a heap of embarrassment. Different abilities might make us proud. But when we ask ourselves unrealistic questions—such as, Why can't my child be mellow and compliant like him? Why can't my child be coordinated like her?—we are feeding our embarrassment and allowing it to gain strength. We are buying into the notion that our children are meant to represent us to the world.

Think back to your early days of parenting or to young parent-child duos that you currently observe in public places. What do you think when a toddler acts up in public? What do you think when a child has a tantrum? Before we had children, we were apt to think that something was wrong—not so much with the child but with the parents. Acting up, tantrums, we thought, must indicate a lack of discipline or parental control. Our future children would never act that way. We simply would not tolerate it.

Ouch! How those thoughts have come back to haunt us. Karen recalls wanting to explain to strangers in the grocery store that she really did not approve of our children's screaming fits, that she had tried everything she could to eliminate them. "It's not my fault!" she felt compelled to shout to those within hearing.

Now that our children are beyond the tantrum stage, we still are not always understanding of parents whose young children behave badly. We ought to be. Most of the time we are empathetic when witnessing situations similar to those we have experienced. But we do find ourselves slipping into those old, familiar patterns of judging parents based on their children's behavior.

Even if we rightly love our child just for being our child, not because of any particular trait or accomplishment, we may still feel a twinge of envy when another parent exercises bragging rights over their child. The twinge increases to a pang if we have no great achievement about which to boast.

But what about when a child's actions bring shame on the parent? Feelings of shame may originate within a parent or be put on a parent by the community—a neighborhood, a church, a town, or even society as a whole. The criminal activity of children presents an extreme example of a source of such parental shame.

We often focus our thoughts and concerns on the families of crime victims. They need our compassion. But think also of the parents of criminals. Yes, a lack of positive parenting is often a factor in pushing people toward crime. But there are many good, caring parents of criminals. The children responsible for school shootings around our country have parents. How do those parents feel? They must live with both ongoing concern for their children and public shame for what their children have done.

Anger

Along with hurting over their children, parents may be angry at them for making poor choices, whether great or small. Concern and anger are not mutually exclusive. In fact, it seems that the more we love, the angrier we may be with our children. Disappointed love can be downright volatile, even venomous: "How could you do this to yourself?" "How could you do this to your family?" "How could you do this to me?" "I warned you, but you wouldn't listen." "I told you things would turn out this way."

It is not uncommon to seek someone—or ones—to angrily blame for the negative circumstances of our children's lives. We may be angry with other people, such as the child's friends, spouse, or boss. We may be angry with institutions—a school, a church, a company—for failing our children. We might think: "If only so-and-so had stood by my child." Or, "If only they had given the right kind of advice." Or, "If only that girlfriend [boyfriend or spouse] hadn't dumped my child, things would be different."

We may be angry with our child's other parent, who may or may not be our spouse, for a whole realm of possible mistakes in relating to the child in trouble. We may accuse the other parent of being too strict or too lenient. We may wish that the other parent had provided a better role model or had spent more or less time with the child.

We may even be angry with God, questioning why certain circumstances befell our child and not others. We are beset by frustrating questions or beliefs: "Did my child deserve this turn of events? Did I?" "It isn't fair!" "Where was God when needed?" "Where were those guardian angels who should have been looking out for my child?" "Other parents, who did no better than I did for my child, have perfect offspring—or at least children without major problems."

Responsibility

As parents of children in trouble and as onlookers, we all seem naturally inclined to want explanations for the causes of children's problems. We try to determine who or what is responsible for the problems.

Aloud or silently, outside observers usually settle on the parents. They reason: "Must not have been proper discipline." "Must not have set the best example." "Must have been some problem in the home." "Must not have been truly godly and righteous."

While we can sometimes trace children's self-destructive actions directly to the actions of the parents (for instance, the son of a drug dealer who grows up to participate in the business), often there is no compelling explanation tying back to the parents for why a child "ends up" in trouble.

But that does not stop the speculation of parental blame. Perhaps judgment of parents by other parents is a form of self-protection. For if onlookers can determine where the errors were made, they may think they can take steps to guarantee that the same does not happen in their families. They can reassure themselves, however falsely, that their children will be safe. By avoiding certain wrong actions, by taking certain other proactive steps, observers may rationalize, there will be a way out for them and for their children. Aside from healthy learning by observation, such reasoning is wishful thinking.

It is bad enough that others blame parents in this manner, but parents themselves commonly take more responsibility for their children's failures than is merited. Even if there are others that we, as parents, can blame, we eventually question our role in the whole scenario. We think: "It must be something I did—or did not do. If only. . . ." Whether we say it out loud or not, inside we feel that we, the parents, must be responsible in one way or another.

Perhaps this tendency is simply the flip side of parents taking too much credit for their children's accomplishments. We ourselves are guilty. Wanting to encourage other parents, we compliment them on the "good job" they are doing with their children. But is the success of their children really a result of their parental efforts or the luck of the draw? Maybe their kids have compliant personalities. Maybe there is not an ounce of resistance in them. Maybe their kids would have turned out great under far less positive parenting. Some do, you know. Or maybe things are not as perfect as they seem.

Surely parental support, encouragement, and discipline increase the odds that a child will do well. But we have all heard the stories of the kids who beat bad odds, who rose above abysmally awful home situations, who broke out of cycles of poverty, crime, even abuse, who made much of their lives in spite of little or no positive parental influence. We are rightly impressed by such exceptional tales.

And what of those other stories, the ones that are not inspirational at all but bring us down, scare us? What of the stories of children who had everything going for them—all the advantages of loving, even Christian, homes, praise, encouragement—but took one or more serious wrong turns and made messes of their lives? Explain that, if you can.

Who is to say that parents of struggling children have not been doing just as good a job parenting as their seemingly successful counterparts? No one, for the fact is that effort does not always equate with success. There are no easy answers. There are no guarantees in this great gamble called parenting. And yet mothers and fathers feel responsible. While we do not want to deny parents of "successful" children their warm feelings of pride, joy, and satisfaction, it seems that parents take too much credit and too much blame for the way their children turn out.

Long-Term Consequences

Sometimes the feelings described above—sadness, embarrassment, shame, anger, and responsibility—gradually lessen and even fade away as parents get used to certain troubling realities regarding their children. If children's problems are eventually turned around, parents' earlier feelings may also turn around. Forgiving and even forgetting can take place, particularly if, so to speak, the prodigal child returns home.

Parents may push down, repress, difficult feelings to enable them to get by. But if parents allow these feelings to remain unaddressed, there is a likelihood that the feelings will deepen, intensify, and surface at inappropriate times.

Sadness to Chronic Grief

Left unaddressed, sadness over a child's ongoing troubling situation can take over and color every aspect of life, robbing parents of all other joy. Unaddressed or repressed sadness can become an all-consuming chronic grief over the child who is "lost."

It can be nearly impossible to live with the daily nagging loss of the child you expected, the child you knew he or she could potentially be. In this unresolved state, the what-ifs and if-onlys can loom large and deepen grief. We naturally question, wondering how and why. Without any answers, we can spiral down into ever deeper grief.

Embarrassment and Shame to Seclusion

Taken to an extreme, embarrassment and shame can lead us to avoid others, even to become reclusive. We hear of parents who avoid events, such as family or school reunions, because they are embarrassed by children's failures (and, apparently, because they expect everyone else's children to be doing well). A woman, for example, stops attending her church because of her son's current drug conviction. She fears being with people who might know about her son's problem, so she stays home. Her sense of shame keeps her reclusive.

Even if parents do not physically seclude themselves from others, they may do so emotionally. They fear entering into conversations that might potentially touch on topics that are most hurtful. They avoid closeness with people whose children appear problem-free. When parents avoid others, when they physically or emotionally lock themselves away, it can be in response to real or perceived judgment, exclusion, or rejection by others.

Our perceptions and projections of how others might respond to us are powerful. They can keep us isolated. But while there are times when hurting parents must isolate themselves in order to heal, a pattern of isolation is self-destructive and only serves to compound one's troubles.

Anger to Bitterness

It is one thing to be angry. It is another to let that anger—whether it is well-founded or misplaced—fester and grow. When this happens, the destructive force of bitterness can go to work inside us. And bitterness is more damaging to the person holding it than to the object of that bitterness. It nibbles away at us. It makes us emotionally and spiritually smaller people and blocks our ability to feel positive feelings.

Just as anger can be directed toward an individual, an institution, or God, so can bitterness. Bitterly blaming others, even shutting them out, is easy to do for parents who struggle to understand why their child has one problem or another. They might think: "I'll never go back to that church. They treated my child so badly that it's no wonder she rebelled." Or, "I never want to see my former daughter-in-law again. I hate her for what she did to my son."

It seems incompatible with parenting, but bitterness toward the very child for whom we ache is not altogether unlikely. In truth, our feelings toward those close to us are usually somewhat mixed. We may develop love-hate relationships with our children who are struggling. Our unresolved bitterness can turn to ever-deepening frustration and resentment toward those children for creating problems and unhappiness for themselves and for us.

Responsibility to Guilt

As parents, most of us have done the best we could for our children. But we all know that parents are not perfect. Some days we are painfully aware of that truth! We have not always provided the best example, communicated clearly, disciplined appropriately, taught thoroughly, or. . . . There may be specific failings that we might regret and that we relate to our children's problems. Whether our parental imperfections have any objective connection to our children's problems or not, we may believe that they do. Though not necessarily logical, this tendency of parents to take responsibility for their children's problems is normal.

Karen often found this to be true of parents with children in medical crisis. Parents would second-guess themselves, wondering what they might have done differently that could have prevented a premature delivery or warded off a birth defect or other medical problem. If they had gotten to the hospital sooner, parents wondered, might the birth have gone better? If they had not fed their child that cereal, would there have been that allergic reaction? If they had recognized delayed motor development earlier, would their child have escaped cerebral palsy? In most cases, there was nothing the parents could have done to alter their children's situations. But parents still asked the questions.

Parents will always be inclined to take responsibility for their children's woes. But taking on responsibility that isn't ours heaps an unnecessarily heavy load upon an already heavy burden. And yet, many hurting parents continue to take the blame for their children's problems.

Remember that parents, children, and their situations are unique. Not all parents whose children fail to meet parental or societal expectations will experience all of the emotions described above. But nearly all troubled parents do experience some degree of disconnection with others, which only compounds their troubles.

Isolation

The hurting parents with whom Karen worked found few others with whom they could honestly relate and share their difficult feelings. While family and friends may have been supportive and helpful in many ways, they did not know what to say or how to say it. Though they tried to be understanding, even those close to the parents found it hard to helpfully relate to them, unless they had been through something similar.

It is a challenge to reach out to a hurting person with genuine empathy without putting one's foot in one's mouth. When children are involved, it seems even more difficult to do so. No wonder! The depth of feeling parents have for their children is unfathomable, causing problems with children to strike at the very core of a parent's being. A hurting parent will likely and understandably be overly sensitive about the subject of their child. Hurting parents also seem predisposed to feel that no one else could possibly understand their pain. And they may be right.

If you have a tiny premature baby who is struggling for life, you can only think that everyone else in the world, everyone you know at least, had strapping newborns who "hit the ground running." Birth is supposed to be normal, natural, easy. But not for you. And not for your infant. What parent of a healthy child could possibly understand such an unnatural situation?

When what is supposed to be a joyful time of experiencing new life and discovery is turned upside down with sickness or death, family and friends may feel threatened. Intentionally or not, they may pull away for lack of knowing how to respond. Consequently, parents in such pain often feel emotionally isolated.

In truth, the hurting parents Karen knew through the support network did not always make it easy for others to relate to them. Some of the isolation these parents experienced was brought on themselves. They withdrew from preexisting relationships and closed themselves off from those who wished to reach out to them. Sharing their pervasive, relentless emotional pain was too much for them. And, truthfully, it was sometimes too much for others to hear. Regardless of the cause, very often parents complained of feeling isolated.

Parents of older children in troublesome situations also often end up feeling isolated. They may reason that no one wants to hear their bad news (and, to a certain extent, this perception might be accurate). They also may feel embarrassed, ashamed, and misunderstood.

In social settings, parents are much more inclined to brag about their children's accomplishments than to discuss their problems. You do not often hear parents telling stories about their children needing to move back home, losing their jobs, struggling to "find" themselves, or experiencing difficulties in their love relationships. But this does not mean their children are free of problems. Although the hurt a parent feels over a child can be very deep, it is seldom discussed with others.

Clearly, there is a great emphasis on conformity in our culture. While we may think that peer pressure applies to only children and adolescents, we adults also are subject to it. Perhaps even more so. We are programmed to try to fit in, to be like everyone else. We typically yield to peer pressure and conform, even though we may be quietly intrigued by those creative and strong enough to be different.

Being left out is tough on a parent's ego. All but the most independent among us want to be included, to be accepted, to be considered normal. We want to have a place in the discussions and activities of other parents. But when our children do not fit the norm, especially when their choices or circumstances place them in significant trouble, there are lots of adjustments for parents to make. Making these adjustments, large or small, can be difficult, as we struggle to discover where we fit among other parents.

In her past work, Karen often observed how the parents of children who were living with challenges—mild cerebral palsy or slight learning disabilities, for instance—did not quite fit in. Like their children, these parents were sometimes marginalized. Play dates were not automatically set and birthday party invitations did not usually arrive for their children, so these parents did not always get to know other parents. There were fewer opportunities for parental socializing on the sidelines or comparing weekend athletic schedules in the grocery store. These parents suffered degrees of isolation just like their children. Inadvertently perhaps, these parents were often ignored by the "typical" parents of "typical" children. And they hurt for their children and for themselves.

It can be much the same for parents of older troubled children. These parents, too, may feel like outsiders in groups of parents with seemingly perfect children. They may always be a bit on edge, hoping the subject of SAT scores or new jobs or grandchildren does not come up.

We may fantasize about baring our souls, admitting to others our children's problems and our difficulties in handling them. But so many doubts can keep us secretive and isolated. We wonder who will *not* flinch when we tell the truth. We wonder who will listen helpfully. We wonder who will walk away and who will stay, be friends with whom we can be who we honestly are, pain and all.

We felt a bit of that isolation years ago. At gatherings, we had often felt what it was like to often be the only people without children. We had witnessed the seemingly obsessive conversations that parents have about their young children. They compared every possible note, going into great detail about birthing experiences, milestones reached, ways to handle everyday challenges, can-you-top-this diapering stories. We each listened with one ear. We did not fully fit in. It was hard to imagine ever becoming so passionate about such seemingly mundane details. Yet we realized that in the future we would likely be joining in such discussions.

After losing our first child, though, we felt more left out than ever. Our need to share our painful parenting experience was just as great as that of the parents who stood around going on endlessly about their little ones. But we had no outlet for expressing what we had been through or how we felt about it. Because of the outcome, ours was not the kind of experience most people would want to hear about. Karen knew what it was like to recover from a cesarean section. She could have gone on and on about that. But we knew most people would not want to hear from a woman who had a cesarean section but no baby. So there was no conversation.

When we buried our child under a spreading oak tree in central Texas, however, in a part of the cemetery reserved for children, we felt a strange comfort. There among the other grave markers, we found what we needed. There, in that place of death, was a club for us. It was a club few ever joined intentionally. But it was, however morbid, just the sort of club we needed. It was made up of people like us—sad, pitiable people whose young children had died.

Of course, we took no pleasure in the loss these families experienced. Our hearts broke for them. But seeing their children's graves, reading the stones with the children's names, knowing that parents had wept over these little lives as we wept over our daughter, reminded us that we were not alone. We had not been singled out. Others had suffered like us. And others had, presumably, gone on with their lives.

Even though we never met these other parents, we found comfort and an uncanny reassurance in knowing that we were not really alone. There is an old expression: Misery loves company. Having been miserable, we suggest a truer variation on that theme: Misery *needs* company.

Thankfully, few parents have to bury their children. But, contrary to public tales of children's successes, most parents do feel degrees of disappointment over unmet expectations. Many of these disappointments are painful. As isolated as you may feel as a hurting parent, you are not really alone. If there were tangible symbols for the losses parents have known, if there were headstones for each disappointment or loss, people could clearly observe that truth.

Forget the Christmas letters overflowing with parental pride. If you could read between the lines of those cheery greetings—or know the stories of those who decided not to send letters this year—you would discover that many other parents hurt as you do. You are, in fact, part of a very large club, but it is one whose membership is largely secret. Call it the Hurting Parents Club. It is far less talked about than the Proud Parents Club. But its membership may be nearly as large, as many parents belong to both clubs.

Now, this may not sound like good news. But if you are feeling isolated as a hurting parent, it can help to know that you are not alone. You and your child have not been singled out for the fate that seems to be only yours. There are many other parents like you also feeling sad, embarrassed, angry, and responsible. They also hurt over the children they love. And along with other parents who might understand your feelings, there is a good God who cares for you. It is a fact: you are not alone in this world of hurt.

Consider Your Feelings and Find Support

1. How do you feel about your child today? Why do you feel this way?

2. How did you feel about your child one year ago?

3. How do you expect to feel about your child one year from now?

4. Who can you talk to about the problems your child is experiencing, as well as your own pain?

5. Do you know any other parents who have children experiencing difficulty? How could you connect with them?

—2—

The Grace of God for Parents

"I will never leave you or forsake you."

—Hebrews 13:5b

W E HAVE CONSIDERED DIFFICULT PARENTAL FEELINGS and their origins, prompting you, perhaps, to reflect on your own hurts over a child. We have been reminded that hurting parents, though often feeling isolated, are not really such a minority after all. While this truth may offer some small comfort, we now want to explore the greatest source of comfort—God.

BLESSING VERSUS GRACE

It would be an unusual hurting parent who had not turned to God with the problems of his or her child. Even those who are not regular prayers admit to pleading with God for their children's health and happiness. If not the very first source of help, God is at least our last resort. After all, desperate times call for desperate measures, and God is who we tend to go to when no one and nothing else seem able to help.

For those already in the habit of conversing with God, prayer certainly becomes more frequent and more fervent when troubled times with children arise. But when the desperately requested resolutions do not come, what then of faith and trust, of confidence in God? At these times, hurting parents can be left feeling more confused, frustrated, and isolated, wondering if God has abandoned them.

For such a dark, upside-down, twisted situation is not at all what we expected. Children are supposed to be a blessing. Think about how often we use the language of blessing in describing children. From the start, we peek in around the blankets at a newborn babe and exclaim, "What a blessing!" We freely describe little ones as gifts, saying that our families are blessed with children. There is even a children's clothing line labeled "Little Blessings." And all this emphasis on children as blessings exists outside of the church.

Within the realm of popular Christianity, the message of children being blessings becomes even stronger. Scripture is quoted to reinforce the belief that children are a blessing from God: "[Children] are indeed a heritage from the LORD, the fruit of the womb a reward. Like arrows in the hand of a warrior are the [children] of one's youth. Happy is the man who has his quiver full of them. He shall not be put to shame when he speaks with his enemies in the gate" (Psalm 127:3-5).

Children who behave well and grow up to obediently follow God, children who are nearly perfect, seem to be God's particular blessings to faithful parents. We like that idea so much that we publicly promote it. As proof of family rewards for righteous obedience to God, we parade the handsome, smiling children (and spouses) of church leaders before congregations.

So what is wrong with this theology? Well, parents who have nearly perfect children usually find nothing wrong with it at all. But for parents with children who have problems, it can seem that children are anything but a blessing. At times, in fact, it can feel like God has cursed both the children and the parents. Are less-than-perfect children a curse from God or, at least, evidence of a withheld blessing? Are their troubling circumstances the result of faithlessness or wrongdoing on the part of their parents? Whether stated or not, this is the implicit, logical counterpart to the theology of blessing.

True, if a parent of a struggling child reads through the wise sayings collected in the book of Proverbs, the message may be disheartening: "Train children in the right way, and when old, they will not stray" (Proverbs 22:6). Which leaves many parents to wearily ask, "How old?" "Discipline your children, and they will give you rest; they will give delight to your heart" (Proverbs 29:17). And from the book of Psalms:

> I have been young, and now am old, yet I have not seen the righteous forsaken or their children begging bread. They are ever giving liberally and lending, and their children become a blessing. Depart from evil, and do good; so shall you abide forever. For the LORD loves justice; he will not forsake his faithful ones. The righteous shall be kept safe forever, but the children of the wicked shall be cut off. (37:25-28)

Like the friends of Job who could not fathom that his misfortunes be anything but punishment for sin, parents, after reading this passage, are left wondering where they went wrong. They may wonder just what they did to merit such punishment. But further biblical reading reveals many accounts of imperfect children, even imperfect children of righteous parents. Children, as well as their parents, have always been imperfect. And God has been in the business of relating to this aspect of the human condition for a very long time.

Think about the first brothers, Cain and Abel, whose story is recorded in Genesis 4. We are not told of Adam's and Eve's responses, but imagine how troubling Cain's murder of Abel must have been for them.

Recall Esau of Old Testament fame. We often think of his twin brother, Jacob, as devious, a trickster who conned Esau out of his inheritance with the help of their mother. But Esau was hardly perfect either, as these verses reveal: "When Esau was forty years old, he married Judith daughter of Beeri the Hittite, and Basemath daughter of Elon the Hittite; and they made life bitter for Isaac and Rebekah" (Genesis 26:34-35).

Consider also the sons of godly Eli the priest: "Now the sons of Eli were scoundrels; they had no regard for the LORD or for the duties of the priests to the people" (1 Samuel 2:12-13a). And continuing in verse 17: "Thus the sin of the young men was very great in the sight of the LORD; for they treated the offerings of the LORD with contempt."

Later in the same book, old Samuel, the holy prophet who judged Israel after Eli's death, made his sons judges over Israel. But the Bible subsequently reports this bad news: "Yet his sons did not follow in his ways, but turned aside after gain; they took bribes and perverted justice" (1 Samuel 8:3).

The sons of King David, Absalom and Adonijah, fought bitterly over succession to their father's throne. And there are others throughout the Old Testament who showed themselves to be far from perfect children, regardless of whether their parents lived righteously.

In the New Testament, Jesus tells the parable of the prodigal son. In this story, the prodigal son demands his inheritance early, as if to say to his father, "I wish you were dead." He then takes his early gotten funds and leaves for a far country. Once there, he squanders his money and sinks so low as to live among the pigs (unclean animals under Jewish law). He eventually comes crawling back to his father to beg for a place as a servant.

The parable, in Luke 4:11-32, includes no hint that the son's misbehavior was a result of any wrongdoing on the part of the parents. As far as we know, they were godly people. And we can assume that they were hurt over their powerlessness to alter the course of their son's life. Instead, they could only wait and watch, hoping to see their child again and be reconciled with him. Do you know of a family— perhaps your own—where parents love their child and are clearly faithful to God, yet their child has problems?

When there are multiple children in a family, there may be one who distinguishes himself or herself as the "black sheep," while the others become model adults. How do you explain that? Yes, there are differences in every parent-child relationship. There are considerations of birth order and gender. There can be emotional or developmental problems. But these explanations only address a few of the causes of drastically different outcomes of children from the same family.

A family Karen knew in her youth made a lasting impression on her when one of the several children became involved with hallucinogenic drugs during college. Although he had stopped his drug use and received psychological help, he remained tormented by terrible flashbacks. Unable to get free of this terror, he took his own life.

It is still hard to understand how this could happen in such a loving family. There were no terrible problems hidden behind the loving public persona of these parents. They themselves struggled to accept their son's choices, to come to some understanding of it all. Their other children have led relatively normal, but varied, lives. One runs the family farm, while another teaches religion at a prestigious university. One set out for adventure afar and became a minister after a deepening experience of faith. They have all had their ups and downs, the kinds of "results" one might expect. But one would never have predicted this family would know the tragedy of a young suicide.

Our own loss of a child has been hard to understand. In the surreal hours between the start of the prenatal stress test and the rushed delivery of our baby, our obstetrician puzzled over just what was happening. When it became increasingly clear that our baby had significant problems, Karen heard our doctor mutter to himself, "This shouldn't happen to such nice people."

This caring man knew we had been trying to conceive a child for longer than one year. While we were not yet desperate, he understood that after ten years of marriage we felt ready. Perhaps he trusted that we would make reasonably good parents. But here we were—a mature, responsible couple, who could not conceive a healthy child and who were about to know the deep pangs of parental loss.

"This shouldn't happen to such nice people." Although the doctor's statement was entirely well-intentioned and even understandable, it still struck Karen as strange. Perhaps it was true that this tragedy should not happen to us. But should it happen to anyone? Do any parents deserve to have their babies born sick and die in their arms? Does any baby deserve to have life cut so short? Surely not.

Do you deserve the pain you are feeling on behalf of your child? No matter whether you have been Parent of the Year or not, it is unlikely you deserve what you are feeling. Does your child deserve his or her struggles? That may be hard to say. Even though some aspects of children's problems may be the consequences of their actions, we must not be quick to judge whether any person deserves his or her fate. Remember Jesus' words, "Let anyone among you who is without sin be the first to throw a stone . . ." (John 8:7).

Once again, our expectations are called into question. If we expect that living our lives right will result in children who will be nothing but blessings to us, we will likely be disappointed. The overarching message of the Bible, despite the promises of the book of Proverbs, is not that blessing is a reward for godly living. It is, rather, that God's grace-filled presence runs through all of life. The good news of the gospel is God's forgiveness and restoration when we—and our children—fail. Yes, we rejoice and count ourselves blessed when all goes well, when our children are healthy, happy, and whole. But we are not cursed when that is not so. It is then, more than ever, that we are in need of the grace of God. And it is there for us.

The phrase *the grace of God* is tossed around freely in Christian circles. But just what is it? *Merriam-Webster* provides this definition:

> unmerited divine assistance given humans for their regeneration or sanctification; a virtue coming from God; a state of sanctification enjoyed through divine grace; approval, favor; mercy, pardon; a special favor: privilege; disposition to or an act or instance of kindness, courtesy, or clemency; a temporary exemption: reprieve.

Grace was a key word in Karen's childhood. Her Lutheran parents taught her about being "saved by grace" rather than good works. Often her father repeated Martin Luther's succinct definition of *grace* as "God's unmerited favor." God's unmerited favor. God's unmerited favor. It was a tiring mantra to a child. But it defines something that we can never have too much of—God's goodness toward us, goodness that we do not and cannot deserve.

The word *grace* is mentioned only a few times in the Old Testament. Strangely, it is not found in the Gospels at all, except as beautifully used in the prologue to John:

> And the Word became flesh and lived among us, and we have seen his glory, the glory as of a father's only son, full of grace and truth. . . . From his fullness we have all received, grace upon grace. The law indeed was given through Moses; grace and truth came through Jesus Christ. (John 1:14, 16-17)

The rest of the New Testament indicates that the early Christian church relied heavily on God's grace, for the word *grace* appears many times, in every book except 1 John and 3 John. *Grace* was in greetings and in parting words, in loving blessings and in theological treatises. Perhaps the abundant use of the word was because of the ever-difficult circumstances of forging something new, of persecution and struggle, of hanging in there, that called for God's grace in great measure. How aware the early followers of Jesus seem to have been of their continual need for God's grace.

The *Nelson NRSV Exhaustive Concordance* tells us that in the Bible grace is used to describe God's favor, God's forgiving mercy, the gospel, gifts such as miracles, and eternal life. It is also the source of many other good things, including salvation, the call of God, faith, justification, forgiveness, and consolation. And it is described as all-abundant, all-sufficient, glorious, great, manifold, rich, and undeserved. (For an excellent contemporary study of the Christian concept of grace, see *Amazing Grace* by Philip Yancey.)

Do any items from this extensive list of definitions and uses of grace strike a chord within you? Do you find yourself in need of consolation? Could you do with a little forgiving mercy? Could you benefit from something all-sufficient? Clearly, any hurting parent needs God's grace.

You have probably heard the phrase, There but for the grace of God go I. In the past, we thought in terms of this saying. Sometimes we would repeat it to each other, especially when we encountered unfortunate souls who were experiencing troubles different or worse than our own. We thanked God that we were not in their shoes! We breathed a grateful prayer, believing that were it not for the merciful hand of God, that could be us. Were it not for God's unmerited favor toward us and our loved ones, we would surely be in trouble.

This view recognizes that our good circumstances are not necessarily of our own making. Others have worked just as hard, been just as good, but have not fared as well. So, we give God the credit for our success and relative happiness. It is God's grace that keeps us from trouble, from poverty, from desperate circumstances.

This belief reflects a humble attitude. There is goodness in crediting God rather than ourselves. It is a simple, easy way of looking at life and explaining the avoidance of suffering. But there is a serious inadequacy with this theology. Think about its implications. What does this say about the grace of God toward those who are not doing well or whose children are not doing well? Has God somehow withheld grace from these others? From you?

There but for the grace of God go I. If this is our interpretation of what happens to us and those around us, we imply the absence of God's grace for those who are afflicted in one way or another. If God's grace makes for good circumstances, then bad circumstances must be the result of some lack of God's grace, of God withholding grace as a form of teaching or punishment.

If we give God credit, it seems that we must also give God blame. Thinking in these terms is confusing and painful. To think that God chooses to shower some with gracious blessing and withhold it from others leaves us with a capricious, heartless God. But this is not the God described in the Bible.

Truly, we can observe in others that much comfort and success is undeserved. And if honest, we can admit the same for ourselves. Likewise, much of the suffering experienced by us and others is undeserved. As parents who hurt, we often ask, whether aloud or silently, why our children should have problems, why they should suffer, why we should be in pain. It doesn't seem fair.

Such questions have no answers. But one thing is certain: Whatever our situation, God does not leave us without grace. Based on the Bible and confirmed by experience, we conclude that God does not withhold grace for any reason. And God's grace does not lessen, is not absent, when we hurt. Quite the contrary. When we struggle—including our struggles as parents—we are in greater need of God's grace. God has compassion for those who hurt, offering "grace to help in time of need" (Hebrews 4:16b).

In light of this life-giving truth, as hurting parents, let's rephrase There but for the grace of God go I, as There *with* the grace of God go I. So, when we walk through the valley of the shadow of death, when we are in the pit, when we hurt, when we struggle, when our children are doing poorly, God's grace is with us, sustaining us through whatever is and whatever may come.

At one time or another, whether in small or large doses, whether seldom or often, we will struggle in life, and we will struggle as parents whose children disappoint and fail. Whether we feel blessed through our children or cursed—or some real-life mixture of the two—God is there with grace.

INCARNATE PRESENCE

Aside from a few principles in the book of Proverbs, the Bible does not promise a perfect life—not for us or our children. What the Bible does promise is that God through the Spirit of Jesus will be with us. "And I will ask the Father, and he will give you another Advocate [or Helper], to be with you forever" (John 14:16). What is so incredibly wonderful about this promise is that we have a God, a God-with-us (this is the meaning of *Emmanuel*) in Jesus, who understands disappointment, suffering, pain. We have with us a God who became a person, taking on all human frailties. Through this incarnation, God joined in our humanity in a unique way.

Perhaps it would have been even more helpful to us as parents had Jesus been a father—or come as a woman and been a mother! Nevertheless, Jesus did gain insight into the suffering of his own parents, particularly Mary, over the choices he made and the circumstances that befell him. He observed other parents. He saw their love and concern. He compassionately raised Jairus's daughter from death (Mark 5:22-24, 35-43). Jesus loved children and drew them to himself:

> Then little children were being brought to him in order that he might lay his hands on them and pray. The disciples spoke sternly to those who brought them; but Jesus said, "Let the little children come to me and do not stop them; for it is to such as these that the kingdom of heaven belongs." And he laid his hands on them and went on his way. (Matthew 19:13-15)

And Jesus did suffer. If not as a parent, he suffered as a child, as a sibling, as a leader, as a friend, as an innocent man falsely accused, convicted, tortured, and executed. Some see one of the shortest verses of the Bible as one of its most powerful: "Jesus wept" (John 11:35). This brief sentence reveals Jesus' humanity, his depth of emotion, his vulnerability. This common experience of grieving unites him with us. Because God became one of us in Jesus, God can empathize with us. God can feel what we feel; God can understand our weaknesses and our pain. And God can comfort us as only one who has been there can.

Karen witnessed this principle on a person-to-person level when she worked with volunteers who counseled troubled parents. These volunteers were all parents who had been there. They had experience with their own medically challenged children and with the isolation that often comes with that territory. Either because other experienced parents had once broken their isolation or because they had never received that gift, they committed themselves to talking with parents newly facing similar circumstances.

The value of such communication and connection between parents was immeasurable. It was a gift that few could give, that money could not buy. To talk with someone who had been there meant the world to hurting parents. That connection made them feel a bit less victimized. It gave them hope and empowered them to move on. The wounds of some became healing medicine for others.

Likewise, but in a deeper, more far-reaching way, our connection with God through Christ is a hopeful, empowering link. With Jesus, who overcame sin, death, and the devil, we can overcome our own demons of parental pain. Having suffered greatly himself, Jesus becomes our wounded healer.

It seems to be human nature that we are best able to receive divine grace when we know—beyond a shadow of a doubt—that we need it. Jesus said that "those who are well have no need of a physician, but those who are sick; I have come to call not the righteous but sinners to repentance" (Luke 5:31-32). When we are injured, when we are sick, when we are grieving, when we have sinned, we need God's healing. Our disappointment in parenting need not be a closed door of failure, but an open door to God's grace in the journey.

In his book *When Faith Is Tested,* Jeff explores the meaning of the apostle Paul's words in 2 Corinthians 12:8-9, where Paul has noted some sort of physical infirmity, his "thorn in the flesh": "Three times I appealed to the Lord about this, that it would leave me, but he said to me, 'My grace is sufficient for you, for my power is made perfect in weakness.'" Jeff offers two explanations for the Lord's words to Paul:

Traditionally, this verse has been taken to mean that our very infirmities provide God with an opportunity to show forth God's sustaining grace. In other words, a person who is able with God's help to tolerate suffering and endure the pain that suffering brings to bear on one is really a kind of witness to the quiet inner resources that come through faith in God. . . . Yet another interpretation . . . might be the following: God's power is displayed in weakness and is made perfect, or complete, in the face of weakness. In fact, weakness is the very channel through which God displays God's power, God's omnipotence. . . . The weakness and vulnerability that [we] deem such an enemy is actually the medium through which God mysteriously displays God's power. God is there in the pain. God is present *in* the hopelessness. God can now be sought in the very chasm of suffering rather than outside it amidst some facade of revivalistic human victory. Suffering has ceased to be only a human experience. God has chosen through the incarnation to make suffering God's dimension also.

God empathizes with hurting people, with hurting parents. The grace that is sufficient for us in our struggles is the empathy of God in Jesus. The power of God that is revealed is the power of empathizing love.

Receiving God's grace in Jesus does not mean that our children—or we—will become perfect. It does mean that we have a strong partner through whatever life brings us. That partner offers forgiveness where we have failed. That partner brings mercy, not judgment, to our pain. That partner brings healing, as only a fellow sufferer can.

Three and one-half years after the April 1994 Oklahoma City bombing, in which 168 people lost their lives, we attended a groundbreaking ceremony for the memorial to be built on the site of the former Murrah Federal Building. Among those present were Vice President Al Gore and Attorney General Janet Reno. Along with six other impressive dignitaries, Reno and Gore spoke of the personal and national horror of the tragedy. More than one speaker made reference to God, to prayer, to healing. For a civic event, there was a strange, but not inappropriate, quantity of religious talk.

Vice President Gore, himself a person of faith, spoke rather openly in religious terms. In remarks meant to comfort and encourage the families of the victims of the bombing, he included the first and last lines of this hymn verse:

> Come, ye disconsolate, where'er ye languish,
> Come to the mercy seat, fervently kneel;
> Here bring your wounded hearts, here tell your anguish:
> Earth has no sorrow that heav'n cannot heal.

Here are the remaining two verses:

> Joy of the desolate, light of the straying,
> Hope of the penitent, fadeless and pure!
> Here speaks the Comforter, tenderly saying,
> "Earth has no sorrow that heav'n cannot cure."
>
> Here see the Bread of Life; see waters flowing
> Forth from the throne of God, pure from above:
> Come to the feast of love; come, ever knowing
> Earth has no sorrow but heav'n can remove.
> (Thomas Moore, Thomas Hastings, Lutheran, #569)

Although we value this hymn of comfort, Gore's quote sounded a dissonant note. Gathered there were several thousand people, among them parents, grandparents, spouses, children, relatives, and friends of the deceased. They had been disconsolate; they had languished; their hearts had been wounded; they had known great anguish. The hymn writer got all that right.

But years after their losses, many of these loved ones were still feeling the sting of their wounds. Their sorrow was heavy. Could heaven heal the senseless act of violence that stole life and love from them? We wondered. Could it heal that here and now? Or only in the hereafter?

Maybe *heal* is not the best word. Better perhaps is the language used with certain cancers, where physicians do not speak of being cured. Rather, they talk of being "in remission." There is a good chance the cancer will never come back. There will be future checkups required. Perhaps some preventive treatment. Though not perfection, *remission* is a good, positive word of hope.

Likewise, the greatest sorrows, over those we love most deeply, may never be cured or completely healed. We will never forget those we love who die. We will never put our hurting children totally out of our minds. But with God's help, we can stop the cancer-like spread of negative emotions that can take over body, mind, and spirit if left untreated.

Rather than promising to make everything perfect, the empathizing, comforting, empowering, incarnate presence of God in Jesus is grace given to suffering parents. With Jesus—who suffered and died for people like us who did not deserve his sacrifice—as our clearest picture of God's grace, we can boldly claim this personal motto: There with the grace of God—there *with* Jesus—go I.

Parental Responsibility

Karen was listening to a television preacher one day while checking out a program on which she was scheduled to appear. The man was saying that we make a mistake when we assume that we can control our lives. He observed that controlling one's circumstances, even one's destiny, seems to be a prominent message these days. Not only is this tenet part of New Age spirituality, but he also rightly associated it with other motivational teaching, including some Christian theology. We are told that if we create and accept a good, right, even godly plan, and then work the plan, everything will turn out as we desire. That is what we are told. And it sounds so good!

But this is not what usually happens. Instead, our plans often get foiled along the way. Sadly, we cannot truly control what happens to us or, contrary to what many parenting books would lead us to believe, to our children.

Some prescribed parenting methods may produce desired results. Hooray! if they work for you. But people, including children, are not entirely predictable. And, despite parents' best efforts at following all the best instructions, children cannot be programmed, and parenting results cannot be guaranteed. The challenge, then, is to acquire the ability to alter our plans, to change course, to become flexible enough, with God's grace, to move around roadblocks and develop new goals. But this requires a vision of life in which we are not in control, but rather trust God as life unfolds.

One of Jesus' parables may help us with this concept. The story of the sower and the seed (recorded in Matthew 13:3-9, with explanation in verses 18-23, and also found in Mark and Luke) illustrates spreading the word of God. The sower scatters the seed of God's word wherever possible. But only that which falls on good soil grows to maturity.

This planting metaphor seems fitting for the parent-child relationship. The same seed of loving parenting sown in various children has entirely different results. Only the seed sown in good soil takes root and grows successfully. Like the sower, the parent is not responsible for the seed's lack of growth. The parent, however, pays a whole lot more attention to the quality of the soil than the indiscriminate sower. We parents often feverishly work the ground, tilling, watering, and fertilizing. And yet, sometimes, we just cannot get the results we seek.

The parent sowing godly values has no promise of how a child will grow up. All the parent can do is faithfully sow the seed, cultivate and nourish the soil, and water and feed the young plant in prayerful hope that it will take root and grow. The final results are not in the sowing parent's hands.

We reject any idea that God holds parents ultimately responsible for how their children turn out. But if parents are not responsible for a child's choices or outcome in life, for what are parents responsible? What does the God of grace, who empathizes with us through Jesus Christ, expect of a parent?

Although we cannot control our children, there are parental responsibilities and personal actions that we can control, by God's grace. These parental responsibilities include the following:

- faithful and unconditional love for each child
- forgiveness of a child for any failures
- personal moral behavior and spiritual habits
- instruction and discipline of a young child
- prayer for a child
- trust in God for a child's future

Let's consider each of these responsibilities more closely.

Faithful and Unconditional Love for Each Child

You already love your child, or you would not be reading this book. The test is to love no matter what. To love when your child fails. To love when your child disappoints. To love when your child's choice runs counter to your own values. To love when you are not allowed to get close. To love when there is nothing but heartache in return.

Karen's mother always encouraged her children to "love the unlovely." Well, our own children can be pretty unlovely sometimes. They can be pretty awful. They can even be unlovable. But we must love them anyway. Difficult as that can be, who else can or will love them unconditionally?

One night years ago, our then preschool daughter bid us good night with this surprising original promise: "I could never stop loving you!" Unconditional love spelled out. (Frankly, we wonder if she came to this conclusion when she was particularly exasperated with us, deciding that she would love us anyway.) Our child's spontaneous words led Karen to this response:

> I could never stop loving you. Whether you become deathly ill, your adorable face is disfigured, you prove to be emotionally unstable, you shave your head, you never go to college, you marry badly or not at all, you go against all that I believe. I could never stop loving you. *(Learning with Molly)*

Isn't this the pledge we want to make to and fulfill for our children? No matter what good or evil they choose, no matter what circumstances come their way, we will stubbornly love them. This was what the prodigal son knew in his heart, and this knowledge allowed him to make his way back home. Henri Nouwen writes, "Whatever [the prodigal son] had lost, be it his money, his friends, his reputation, his self-respect, his inner joy and peace—one or all—he still remained his father's child" *(The Return of the Prodigal Son)*.

We have all heard the expression, A face that only a mother could love. There are times when, no matter how beautiful or handsome they may be, our children are tough for even a parent to love. Then we must rely on God's grace working in and through us. As God through Jesus loves us without condition, we strive to love our children.

Forgiveness of a Child for Any Failures

Just as we are forgiven by God for our parenting failures and all other sin, we need to forgive our children for any errors of their ways. When children make painful choices, it is usually not with malice toward parents. When Jeff was growing up, his exasperated father would occasionally exclaim, "You're just doing that to get me!" Though seldom true, it can seem that way to parents at times.

Parenting is hard work, physically at first and emotionally later. It is a demanding lifelong job with no guaranteed results, probably life's greatest gamble. Somewhere along the way, every parent has felt unappreciated. It is hurtful for parents to think that despite everything they've done for their children, their opinions could be thrown aside, their values disdained or their feelings ignored. Hardest of all may be forgiving our children for pain they are causing us through ingratitude, insensitivity, or intentional action.

When their choices and behaviors negatively impact us, we especially need to forgive our children. And we need to forgive them whether they ask for our forgiveness or not, as the prodigal son's father demonstrated:

> The boy is back, that's all that matters. Who cares why he's back? And the old man doesn't do what any other father under heaven would have been inclined to do. He doesn't say he hopes he has learned his lesson or I told you so. He doesn't say he hopes he is finally ready to settle down for a while and will find some way to make it up to his mother. (Frederick Buechner, *Telling the Truth*)

No, this father throws a party. Now that's forgiveness! What a dramatic picture of God's forgiveness of us all and a model of parental compassion.

Personal Moral Behavior and Spiritual Habits

Our consistent, personal example of following God's ways will be the greatest testimony to a child of how to choose well and live wisely. Actions do speak louder than words. And a big part of that example will be in how we weather the storms in our own lives, how we cling to God when the going gets tough. Our children will need to witness that kind of dependence on God in preparation for their tough times.

Observable spiritual activities such as church attendance, prayer, and Bible reading will strengthen us as well as provide a positive example for our children. These disciplines can be vehicles to bring God's grace to us, empowering us to face all of life, the good times and the bad. Richard Foster's *Celebration of Discipline* is an excellent resource to guide us in the disciplines of the Christian faith. There are many other worthwhile books that can encourage our faith development and spiritual practices.

Our own attitudes of respect, honesty, generosity, and self-control—both within the family and beyond—will speak volumes to our children. And it is not too late to begin to display these habits and attitudes. In fact, if you sense a personal need to grow in some of these areas, it may well be that the positive changes that take place in you will capture the attention and curiosity of your child.

Instruction and Discipline of a Young Child

Although the results are not predictable, it is primarily the parents' responsibility to teach their children about faith and values. Some of this we do personally, and some we may expect from Sunday school teachers and youth leaders, from others in whose care we place our children. In his book *Lost Boys*, James Garbarino claims that "supportive religion" reduces teen suicide and depression, as well as casual sex and substance abuse.

Some of our instruction involves boundaries of behavior. People of all ages need boundaries. Through adolescence, those boundaries, and appropriate consequences for crossing them, are best established by parents. We parents need God's wisdom in determining the standards of discipline for the different ages of our children and the stages of their development. As our children grow up, however, we tend to lose the role of disciplinarian in their lives. They must learn self-discipline. And they learn it based, in part, on the boundaries we set for them in their early years and on our own personal examples of self-control.

An April 1999 Partnership for a Drug Free America report states that "teens who had discussed drugs with their parents were 42 percent less likely to use drugs than teens whose parents had avoided the subject." In addition, "48 percent of parents reported talking with their children at least four times about drugs in the past year." But "only 27 percent of teens interviewed recalled regular conversations about drugs with their parents." We offer this example to indicate that parental input into a child's life, communicating about difficult subjects that young people face, does have a positive impact. Yet only a minority of parents do so, and even fewer children recall such conversations. It seems that parents must talk with their children about important, even difficult, issues openly and often.

Maybe you have taught your child about God and about appropriate behavior, and perhaps you have provided healthy discipline along the way, but your teaching doesn't seem to have entirely "taken." Hope that the word of God that has been planted within your child will sustain through difficult times and bear fruit in the future. Perhaps you did not provide such instruction and discipline when your child was younger. That is regrettable, but by God's grace you can forgive yourself and move on. There may be future opportunities, even with "older" children, to graciously offer your wisdom and experience (but remember that few adults take well to being explicitly told what to do by their parents).

Prayer for a Child

If praying for your child is something you have not done consistently over the years, it is not too late. Now would be the perfect time to start. Pray when things are good for your child. Pray when things are bad. But for what will you pray? For success or for peace? For money or for satisfaction? For popularity or for a true friend? Consider not placing so much value on the outer trappings of what might define a good life for your child, not so much on what would look like success to you and your social circle. Rather, consider the deepest needs that your child might have, and ask God to meet them with grace.

While you are at it, pray for yourself, that God would help you to love and accept, understand and embrace your child. Pray that God would give you wisdom to know just how to help, when to reach out and be involved and when to pull back.

Trust in God for a Child's Future

As much as we love our children, God loves them even more. God is gracious and merciful. Do not give up on your child, but do work on relinquishing the control you may be trying to have over your child. Give that child up to God.

Participants in Alcoholics Anonymous and other Twelve-Step programs have a number of mottoes for living healthy lives. We've all heard, One day at a time, for instance. Here's another that can be especially helpful to a struggling parent: Let go and let God. For we parents are not God. And we are not responsible for our children's lives.

To some of us, this is a shocking announcement. But we are mere mortals who cannot truly control the courses of our children's lives. This may sound like bad news. But it is meant to be freeing, to help us recognize our true responsibilities and to let go of the rest.

It is God who shows us how to accomplish the parental responsibilities that are in our control. It is God who is the model in Jesus. It is God who provides the strength and grace to follow through. But just as no child is perfect, there are no perfect parents. We parents sometimes fail in one or many of our responsibilities. And rightly or not, we may relate some of our parenting failures to our children's problems. But when we mess up as parents, God forgives us. And we can expect God's grace for us and our children. While there are consequences for parenting mistakes, God can mend what we tear. With God's help, we can do our best, as most of our parents did for us. Lord knows, they were not perfect. And neither are we. But we go on with God's grace.

Consider the Grace of God for You

1. Do you feel that your child is a blessing to you? Why or why not?

2. When you think about your child, how do you feel toward God?

3. Does it help you to think of God suffering with you?

4. How can you sense God's presence in your life, especially in your struggles as a parent?

5. Can you relinquish your sense of being responsible for making your child perfect? If yes, how so? If no, why not?

6. Which of the parental responsibilities on page 45 might you need to take on?

—3—

Receiving Grace and Passing It on to Our Children

In hope that sends a shining ray
Far down the future's broadening way,
In peace that only thou canst give;
With thee, O Master, let me live.

—Washington Gladden

KNOWING IN OUR HEADS and believing in our hearts that God freely gives us grace to make it through our days is one thing. Appropriating that grace—accepting and applying it—is another. For the troubled times of parenting, the grace of God must be more than a concept.

God's grace in action can allow us to accept ourselves and to accept our children, despite failures. That amazing grace can enable us to go beyond acceptance to embracing our children as they are. As we learn to focus less on the pain of what ought to be, we can move on in life and stop defining ourselves in terms of our children. And we may even find that through it all we can grow in significant ways.

ACCEPTANCE

If we can accept God's grace for us personally—that God loves us and is always with us, that God offers us compassion in our dark times—we can better accept ourselves as children of God, as imperfect parents of imperfect children. For starters, we may need to seek God's forgiveness as parents, whether we are in any way "to blame" for our children's failures or not.

King David prayed that God would "clear [him] from hidden faults" (Psalm 19:12b). Perhaps you wonder whether you always did and said the right things with your child. Perhaps you worry about what you "should" have done but did not. Perhaps you wish you had known and taught more about God in your home. For any and all shortcomings on your part, God is ready to mercifully forgive.

If we cannot shake our guilt for any of our failings, we need to be freed to forgive ourselves. Beyond confessing to God, this may require confessing to our children and asking for their forgiveness.

Wiping the slate of the past clean will not necessarily undo the effects of what we have done and have not done, but it can clear our consciences, facilitating self-forgiveness. As we place the totality of our lives in God's merciful hands, let us seek God's forgiveness and ask that God help us to forgive and accept ourselves as parents:

> *Gracious God, how inadequate I feel as a parent. There is so much I wish I had said or done, and so much I wish I had not. By your mercy, forgive me now. And help me to forgive myself. In the future, guide and strengthen me to be a better parent. May my words and actions be channels of your love and care for my child. And may I forgive as you forgive me. Amen.*

By accepting ourselves as imperfect, we will be better able to accept our children as they are. Having humbled ourselves to receive God's mercy, perhaps we will see our children as people equally in need of God's grace.

Growing up, Karen repeatedly heard that one should hate the sin but love the sinner. As not all struggling children are in trouble as a consequence of their own sin, we might modify this advice: Hate the situation, but love the child. That is our challenge in accepting our imperfect children as they are.

While we parents can never truly achieve God's perfect, unconditional love in our relationships, we can remind ourselves that the Heavenly Parent loves everyone, always, no matter what. God's faithful, constant love continues even for those who repeatedly err in their actions and inactions. And many stories in the Bible relate God's love to us. According to Henri Nouwen, "More than any other story in the

Gospel, the parable of the prodigal son expresses the boundlessness of God's compassionate love" (*The Return of the Prodigal Son*). Many hymns also reinforce the nature of God's love, as this old text so eloquently exemplifies:

> There's a wideness in God's mercy,
> Like the wideness of the sea;
> There's a kindness in his justice,
> Which is more than liberty.
>
> There is welcome for the sinner,
> And more graces for the good;
> There is mercy with the Savior;
> There is healing in his blood.
>
> But we make his love too narrow
> By false limits of our own;
> And we magnify his strictness
> With a zeal he will not own.
>
> For the love of God is broader
> Than the measure of man's mind;
> And the heart of the Eternal
> Is most wonderfully kind.
> (Frederick W. Faber, Lutheran, #493)

We can carry God's love into the relationships we have with others, especially our children. As an expression of God's broad love, we need to learn to love our children as they are and love them more than we love the dreams we have for them. Whatever perfect dream you have for your child, there is at least a part of it that you must give up. If you do not let go of that dream, you will waste your days loving your dream-child more than the child you have.

As part of the process of letting go of that dream-child, those initial expectations, we might consider the basis of that first dream. What values of ours shaped that dream? Was our lost dream based in reality or on society's view of perfection, some ideal image we had unquestioningly accepted?

We need to realistically examine our expectations. For starters, how important to us is our children's financial success? That is a tough one, as "money makes the world go 'round." Surely we want our children to be financially independent and enjoy a degree of security. But could we accept children who do not make much money by choice, ability, or circumstance? Could we accept that a child might, for instance, want to pursue an artistic vision rather than get a "real job"?

While living in California's Silicon Valley years ago, we were acquainted with many nouveau riche parents in our church who had achieved great professional and financial success. Their achievements, however, posed a problem for the next generation. How could their children exceed those successes, as previous generations had successively done? It was highly unlikely that these children would do better than their parents had. Even equaling the parents' level of achievement was improbable.

What's more, the children of these corporate leaders, these scientists, these entrepreneurs, these real estate magnates, might not have wanted to do similar things with their lives. One adult child of a top scientist wanted to be a firefighter. Another child of a real estate tycoon wanted to paint houses and trim trees. Neither child was sailing through college. And they had no plans for graduate school. Their parents were disappointed.

But, based on honest assessment of their abilities and desires, perhaps these children made totally appropriate choices for them. Maybe the children had seen the downside of the mega–rat race their parents had bought into. Maybe they wanted jobs or careers that would allow them more time with their families. Maybe these children were not so foolish after all.

Besides wealth, on what else do we base our views of success and perfection? Outwardly, there is the matter of generational taste. When we were adolescents, it was long hair on boys that concerned parents. Today's parents of teenagers may be uncomfortable with shaved heads or spiky, dyed hair, excessive body piercing or tattoos, or with certain clothing styles. We would be much more comfortable if our children would mimic our fashion choices, wouldn't we?

While outward appearance can sometimes indicate more than a fashion statement and harmless rebellion, our emphasis on looks that conform to our own tastes can be blown out of proportion. Being uncomfortable with a style or embarrassed by our child's appearance begs the question of how much emphasis we place on appearance rather than substance.

With the exception of celebrities, who may be admired and rewarded for their unconventional, wild ways, society tends to value conformity in personality, attitude, thinking, and behavior. We saw evidence of this early on in the ways in which others responded to our children. For instance, the same woman taught both our children in a preschool program for three-year-olds. Our older child, who was in the program three years before her brother, did not much care for being at the school. But the teacher praised her for her compliance and cooperation. It didn't matter that her good behavior was motivated more by fear and nervousness than anything else.

Our younger child, who enthusiastically ran into the twice-weekly class, was, surprising to us, labeled as "difficult." He was outgoing and fun-loving, with both a need for interaction and stimulation. But that was not the expected, desired behavior. That was not what was valued. That was not what worked best for the teacher and other adults in charge. Instead, they preferred quiet compliance, no matter its motivation.

As parents, we, too, may prefer a certain personality type. One kind of child may mesh better with our own personalities and our goals, while another—whether like us or very different—might naturally clash with them. But we cannot choose these combinations, can we? And what we expect, what we want, what we think would be ideal, may be anything but. The child we might automatically label as "difficult" might be the one who is most creative, who has the greatest potential for new thought, for bold action, for rich living, for unashamed giving. The child who might be labeled as "good" could be the one who is dull and empty of original thought, who someday might go along with others less benevolent, the same way he or she goes along with us. Conformity in the classroom or at home, so desired by the adults in charge, can squelch creativity and the best aspects of individuality.

Years before we had children, friends sternly corrected us. We had innocently remarked that their young child was "such a good boy," or we had responded to some action of his with "good boy." No! We were never to use that language again. For several reasons. First, all children, the couple reminded us, are good. Not one of them is bad. Second, goodness is not based on behavior, on one action or another. And third, children, the couple believed, do not choose their personalities, with some deciding to be easygoing and cheerful and others deciding to be more difficult.

Maybe our friends were a bit picky and overly quick to correct us. But we saw then—and even more so after we became parents— that they were so right. If a "good baby" is the one who sleeps through the night, never fusses, keeps to a schedule, and smiles and coos (as if the child were deciding to behave this way!), then it follows that the inconsolable child must be a "bad baby." Wrong. We may think using such expressions is just a matter of semantics, merely a harmless activity where meaning is understood in context. But words are powerful, and they can belie our actual perceptions and feelings. Words are so powerful that they can become self-fulfilling prophecies, labels our children come to believe about themselves.

While our children are infants and forevermore, we parents must be careful not to label them in terms that are limiting, one-dimensional, derogatory, and even unfairly positive. Doing so attributes inherent value based on behavior—good, bad, easy, difficult— not the person. We must be on the lookout for stuffing our children in boxes they may not rightly fit for our own convenience, remaking them into images that we—and society—have for them. The pressures on us to mold and label are great. That is what society demands, that is what makes things easier for all involved, that is what we as parents are trained and expected to do. But this ignores individuality and ties our worth as people too closely to particular personalities, talents, and actions.

Our children's love relationships are another important category of parental expectation. Most parents want and expect their children to marry happily and have their own children (our *grandchildren*). This is a reasonable and loving parental expectation. But, whether by choice or circumstance, our children may not marry. If they do, the choice may not be made according to our taste or our timetable. For some, their choice to marry may result in blended families, complicated by exes, steps, and halves. And for many, with a national divorce rate hovering at 50 percent, painful family break-ups are likely.

As we come to terms with the dreams we once had for our children, we may see that they are based on materialism, on the standards set by our social circles, perhaps even on our desires to appear successful to others. In relinquishing old dreams, we may have to reconsider what matters most. We may find that list to be much shorter than we once would have believed.

Accepting ourselves and examining the roots of our dreams will help us to give our children the grace-filled gift of accepting them as they are. But to truly accomplish this we may also have to accept—though not necessarily approve of—their current situations. We may need to stop denying to ourselves and others just what is going on. Even if we "hate the situation," we may have to move beyond hating the people involved.

To live in the reality of the present, rather than the dream of the past or the wishful thinking of the future, may require further forgiveness on our parts. Even when others are rightfully to blame for our children's situations, hanging on to bitterness and blame only compounds our pain and prevents our acceptance of things as they are. Forgiveness is the only way we know to prevent such bitterness. Again, we can look to Jesus as our source and model of grace and mercy.

Jesus prayed on the cross of his execution, "Father, forgive them; for they do not know what they are doing" (Luke 23:34). "They" may not have known that they were condemning, mocking, torturing, nailing, piercing the Son of God. But they knew that they were tormenting and killing another man. And they even may have known the man was innocent. Yet Jesus forgave them and even asked his heavenly Father to do the same.

Has someone wronged your child—in school, in a relationship, in business, through a criminal act? It is terrible. It should not have happened. But unless you can forgive, you will be bound by bitterness.

Not only is Jesus our example of forgiveness, but he also is the source of the strength necessary to make forgiveness part of our lives. And we need his strength, for forgiveness is often difficult to grant. When it comes to hurts against our children, it is harder than ever.

Pray that God will release you from bitterness. Pray that God will allow you to exercise wide mercy. Pray that God will give you the

strength to forgive as Jesus does—toward self, child, and others—
completely and forever.

EMBRACING

Acceptance of our children—with their warts, wounds, and all—is
good. It is necessary. But it is only a first step. To be happier, to be
released from slavery to our pain, we parents must move beyond
acceptance.

Mary, mother of Jesus, seems to have accepted the fact that
her son was different from the rest of the children. She had been
told this from the beginning. (And if she really was a virgin while
pregnant with Jesus, she surely knew that her son was special.) But
even though she had been told and believed that Jesus was different, she must have had unmet expectations. Surely she worried
about him. Surely she wondered if his choices were the right and
best ones.

Although we speak of Jesus as sinless, as perfect, he was hardly
perfect by the standards of the world. He never married. And the
Gospels are not clear about whether or not he had a home of his own
or ever held a job. Eventually Jesus, on the outs with the religious and
legal establishments, suffered a most shameful, torturous public execution. How did Mary explain that to her relatives and neighbors?
Jesus was a special, one-time case. But still we wonder, how did Mary
move from merely accepting Jesus as different to embracing him as
he was?

We faced this on a small scale with our older child, who was
strong-willed or, as some say, "spirited." For several years, we thought
we could mold and shape her into the person we thought she ought
to be, into the image of perfection we had for her. For instance, Jeff
imagined that his little girl would smile sweetly back at those parishioners who fussed over her at church. She would interact positively
with them—and maybe inadvertently enhance his ministry!

Not a chance. After a while, we realized that no amount of coer-
cion on our part would make our child sociable. She was who she
was, and that was that. Giving up on changing her, we gradually
began to accept the unsociable aspect of our child's personality.

When we accepted this reality, we were better able to see the many positive aspects of her personality, to appreciate her enough to truly embrace the unique individual that she is.

Karen has seen this acceptance process many times with parents of children with disabilities. Although the process, in her experience, can be slow and perhaps never complete, a transition must be made to embracing one's child as he or she is. Acceptance allows parents to appreciate, embrace, and love the unique individuals their children are. It also helps parents replace lost dreams. Accepting and embracing our children is a gift for both us and them.

We would not want to minimize your child's problems or your concerns. But whatever negative characteristics may be evident in your child, there are positive, unique qualities there as well. What is positively special about your troubled child? A great deal, most likely. Our strong-willed, noncompliant child is very bright. Her brainpower is special. Our child who will not settle down meets life with exuberance.

When we recently met the teenage child of friends, we were surprised. This boy, from a young age, had been involved with drugs and had run-ins with the law. From time to time, he would disappear from home for days. He had dropped out of high school. He had been alcohol- and drug-free for several months when we met him and was participating in Alcoholics Anonymous. This was not, however, the first time he had gotten sober. Everyone, especially his parents, hoped and prayed it would be the last time he would need to.

What was so surprising about this young man was how charming, bright, articulate, passionate, and insightful he was. We found it hard to imagine all the trouble he had been in and had caused his parents. But the very traits we found so appealing were probably some of the same ones that led him astray. Two sides of the same precious coin. Intelligence led to boredom with school; passion opened the door to experimentation; and charm enabled him to con his parents and teachers.

For better and for worse, every child is unique. The human package is never all good or all bad. It is not healthy, helpful, or loving to accept just parts of each other, only parts of our children. We must embrace the whole mixed bag. And yet it is such a common tendency for us to want to change those we love and not truly love them fully until they change. Our relationships with our children cannot afford our withholding of complete love. Whether the changes that we pray for our children ever come about or not, we are called to love them as they are, to surrender in the battle to change them, to give up our old dreams for them, to open our arms wide in a full embrace.

In most cases, there are chances for us to create new dreams for our children to replace the ones we have been forced to discard. Even children's adversity may give rise to their learning and growth and to our development of positive new dreams for them.

The parents of one of Karen's friends never wanted to see their daughter become a single parent. When her husband told her he wanted out of their marriage, they hurt badly for her. They hated to see her rejected and struggling. They had dreamed that their daughter would marry and live happily ever after, that her children would always know mother and father living in love under the same roof. This is a nice dream. But, in reality, the marriage had not been all that great. And while the balance of blame for the marital difficulties seemed to lie with the woman's husband, her own communication style in the home was largely ineffective. Her sense of self-worth was low, and she allowed herself to be dominated by her controlling husband. She shrank as a person of value within her own household.

This woman's parents would rather that she had been able to improve the relationship and stay married. That would have been her choice as well. But that dream was not to be. A new dream had to be created to take its place. The new dream was that this woman would become a strong single parent, that she would be resilient, that she would grow into self-sufficiency, that she would come to see herself as a person of worth and value, that she would be more assertive and communicate more effectively. And all of that has come true, along with a relationship with God that has grown immeasurably. In this case, the new dream is not so bad after all.

For others, the dream may have been to have children who stayed drug-free through life. When teenage experimentation started, that dream had to be altered. Perhaps the new dream was for these children to not get addicted and to stay "out of trouble." But suppose some of these children go to prison for selling drugs. Their parents' new dream might be that their children will turn around while incarcerated, become successfully rehabilitated, and choose a different life upon release.

One way to alter a dream is to stop comparing. Again, your child is unique. Your child's circumstances are also unique, even if they parallel those of others. And your relationship with your child is unique. Comparing with others is unconstructive. It serves no good purpose for you or your child. You are not that other parent with that other child with those other circumstances. The situation before you is entirely different. Maybe it didn't have to be this way. Maybe things could have been like someone else's more positive situation. Maybe, but you must accept your reality. To move beyond regret and frustration over what should have been, what could have been, you will need to give up that old dream. And this will not be easy. You may be painfully reminded of your unfulfilled dream as you see it happily fulfilled in the lives of others. But if you can minimize comparing yourself to others, you will be better able to embrace what is and begin to dream a new dream for your troubled child.

The good news is that while we cannot change others, including the child for whom we are concerned, we do have some degree of control over ourselves. And changing our dreams does require changing ourselves. We may have to be creative in replacing old dreams with new ones. We may have to come up with new interests, new desires. We may have to search our souls for what really counts, again questioning our own values and their sources.

Forming new dreams for our children may demand forming new dreams for ourselves. Perhaps, for example, we dreamed of spending time with grandchildren and helping them grow up. Instead, we may have the challenging opportunity to get to know and influence teenage step-grandchildren. Perhaps we dreamed of teaching a child to run the family business. Instead, we may put time and money into helping that child recover from financial failure. Perhaps we imagined sharing our child's success stories with the bridge club. Instead, we may become active participants in a recovery community.

This process of embracing our children as they are and of developing new dreams for them is more easily proposed than accomplished. But we have the promise of God's guiding grace as we navigate such stormy seas.

MOVING ON

Studies and casual observation indicate that most men are defined, by themselves and by others, in terms of what they do. What is their job, their title, their position? Women, by contrast, typically define themselves in terms of their significant relationships. Wife, mother, sister, daughter, friend. With more women working outside the home and more men assuming greater roles within the family, this distinction in self-definition may change over time, but for now it still remains generally true.

Jeff's present congregation has a large population of people who are older than sixty. Observing these people, it seems that retired men begin to shift their focus away from what they formerly did in their careers toward who they are related to—their wives, children, and grandchildren. As they move on into old age, they become very sentimental about their families, even more so than their wives. Getting closer to death, they seem to view their offspring as a far greater legacy than whatever they did for employment. And they frequently regret that they did not put more effort into those relationships in earlier times. It seems that they hone in on what really counts, the people they love.

So what are you? How do you define yourself? Being mother or father is undoubtedly a big part of your identity. But as important as relationships are—surely more important than what we do—it is always dangerous to define ourselves in terms of someone else. Through death, illness, divorce, distance, estrangement, or just plain growing up, that person on whom we base our self-definition may not always be there for us. What then? Who are we without that person?

On a snowy walk around the block on the day after her Christmas miscarriage, Karen asked herself, "Can I be happy, can I be whole, if I never become a parent?" It had been twenty-six months since we had decided to try to have a baby—not very long compared to what some couples endure. But during that time, we experienced more than twelve months without conception, then eight months of pregnancy, followed by the death of our newborn child, and then this early miscarriage. Things were not looking good in the baby department. Thinking and praying on her lonely, cold, gray walk, Karen answered her own question, "Yes, with God's help."

Maybe that was an easy answer, since the potential for parenthood, natural or adoptive, was still great. But Karen felt very strongly at that moment that God was reaffirming that with or without a child of her own, she was still God's child. She was well-loved and cared for, important in her own right, not needing any other particular relationship, even that of mother and child, to be complete. And she sensed a tremendous and powerful freedom in reaching this conclusion.

So what about *after* having become parents? To what extent do our children define us? Where is that fine line between caring completely for one's child and not being defined so much by "parent" as by "person"? Just as children must accomplish psychological self-ideation, realize that they are separate beings from their mothers (or primary caretakers), we parents must realize we are separate beings from our children. For many parents, this happens gradually over time. For some, this happens when the child goes to kindergarten. For others, this realization does not come until, following their children's high school or college graduation, the "nest" is empty. Regardless of timing, parents have to let go of their children and of defining themselves in terms of their children. It is not easy. We have to admit that our children are their own people, free to make their own choices and mistakes.

It has been said that parents are only as happy as their least happy child. This maxim rang so true the first time we heard. Again and again, we had seen evidence of unhappy parents of unhappy children: The eyes of some parents moistening as they sang hymns. The reluctance of parents to discuss their children in any depth. The general heaviness of spirit reflected in pervasive sadness. All of this made the saying seem entirely too true.

From one perspective, the maxim reads as an inescapable curse, or at least a dark prophecy—one that would make any parent selfishly pray even harder for his or her children's happiness. Family ties are strong. As strong as the attachment is between parent and child, as deep as emotions run in parents concerning their children, the above statement makes perfect sense. But, realistically, does it have to be true? If our children are unhappy for life, does this doom us to a life of misery? Is unhappiness necessarily the lot of parents whose children are unhappy?

Without the grace of God, perhaps so. But the grace of God can allow us to appropriately detach, to move on. Moving on does not mean leaving our children behind, but being free, by the grace of God, to be whole persons in spite of the pain of someone we love. Admittedly, this could be seen as a kind of compartmentalizing: When I am at the grocery store, I will not think about my troubled child. When I am socializing with my friends, I will not focus on the fact that my child is hurting. I will make boxes of my life and put the hurt concerning my child in one or two of them and not allow that hurt to seep into the other boxes.

The mother of a victim of a terrorist bombing put the loss of her child this way: "It's like an amputation." A part of her—a most important part, like an arm or a leg—had been brutally removed forever. Every day for the rest of her life she would be reminded of what she had lost. But this mother added that an amputee can go on to have a life despite loss.

While most parents will not have to deal with death of their children, they still struggle with loss. They may still feel, whether always, for a period of time, or from time to time, like a part of them, a vital part, has been severed. So let's return to the comparison to the amputee.

Compartmentalizing may not be easy for the amputee. After time, there may be moments when the missing limb is forgotten. But mostly, the amputee must live with his or her loss minute by minute, must come to terms with it at each challenge. The loss is incorporated into life. One can never forget. But unless the person accepts the loss and comes to define themselves as more than an amputee, emotional life and health will be severely limited.

Just as those with disabilities do not want to be wholly defined as "disabled," do not want to be summed up in a word or phrase, hurting parents do not benefit from defining themselves as merely "hurting parents." Though emotions of parenting are strong and consuming, we must not define ourselves totally in terms of our children. This is unhealthy enough when all is well, but when children are imperfect, it can be devastating.

So who are you, if not primarily a parent of a troubled child? You are a precious child of God. You are loved for who you are. You are forgiven your mistakes and sins. You are supported in your struggles. You are comforted in your loss and sorrow. God is with you every step of the way. With God, you can move on through whatever today and tomorrow bring.

Moving on does not have to be merely getting by, dragging yourself through one day to another. With God's grace, there is a supernatural potential for inner peace that would not naturally fit with our trying circumstances. By rights, we ought to be distraught over our children when they are experiencing significant trouble. We are parents who love. Pain is thus inevitable. But, as Paul shows us in Philippians 4:6-7, it need not hold us captive:

> Do not worry about anything, but in everything by prayer and supplication with thanksgiving let your requests be made known to God. And the peace of God, which surpasses all understanding, will guard your hearts and your minds in Christ Jesus.

We have permission and encouragement to bring our troubles to God. In return, we are not promised that all will suddenly be changed to fit our desires. But we will have a heavenly peace that is larger than our pain—a peace that surpasses human sense—and helps us through our earthly struggles.

GROWING

Living through another person is not healthy. Oh, living through one's child can feel pretty good—if the child is doing admirably, if all is well. We may vicariously experience successes that have never been ours personally. We may reap some of the benefits of our children's education, their careers, their status, their finances, their fame, their exciting times. Buoyed by them, we can stay young and on top of the world. But the rub comes when that other life hits some bumps, when it meets with distress or failure. What then? Living life painfully through one's child is self-defeating.

The alternative is not to totally separate our lives from our children's lives. We are parents and we will always want to be closely connected with them. But we need a more positive and practical alternative, for both good times and bad. That alternative is to be vulnerable enough to learn and grow by way of our children. By observing them, by looking and listening with eyes and ears open, we can learn some amazing lessons of life and faith. And this strategy helps us to unhook, too. No longer do we have to be the teachers, feeling responsible for the successes (or failures) of our children-students. We can be the learners, absorbing the lessons our children bring our way.

Just before telling the parable of the sower, Jesus, in answering why he spoke to his disciples in parables, repeats a portion of the prophet Isaiah's words (Isaiah 6:10) to them:

> "You will indeed listen, but never understand, and you will indeed look, but never perceive. For this people's heart has grown dull, and their ears are hard of hearing, and they have shut their eyes; so that they might not look with their eyes, and listen with their ears, and understand with their heart and turn—and I would heal them." (Matthew 13:14-15)

Then Jesus concludes: "But blessed are your eyes, for they see, and your ears, for they hear. Truly I tell you, many prophets and righteous people longed to see what you see, but did not see it, and to hear what you hear, but did not hear it" (Matthew 13:16-17).

The extent to which we see and hear and understand God's word, the extent to which we comprehend Jesus himself, will depend in large part on our hearts, on our attitudes, on our willingness to see and hear and understand. Likewise, the extent to which we learn from our children will depend on what we are looking for. If we are only concerned with changing them and their circumstances, we will miss much of what is offered through them for our change and growth. When we tune in to the lessons God has for us through our children, what we can gain by way of their good times and bad, is limitless. Karen wrote of this in *Learning with Molly,* specifically regarding young children. But parental learning does not have to stop as children get older. Growth through our children can continue as long as we will allow it.

When our children are doing poorly, some of the lessons that we learn from them will be extremely difficult. We have already shared the early parenting lessons bestowed on us through the illness and death of our infant daughter. Our own healthy, living children have showered us with countless more lessons. We are certain that they will go on doing so for as long as we live.

This is not to say that you must have children to learn God's lessons. Truly, if we are open to seeing and hearing God in all our varied experiences, we will notice much that otherwise might pass us by. But the intensity with which we parents feel does open us up to great vulnerability and potential teachableness through our children. What an awesome—and sometimes awful—opportunity is ours to learn and grow as parents.

CONSIDER EMBRACING YOURSELF AND YOUR CHILD

1. What about your child is difficult to accept or embrace?
2. What about your child is wonderful?
3. What dream(s) for your child have you had to give up?
4. What new dream(s) can you dream for your child?
5. Besides being a parent, who are you?
6. If your child has problems, how does that change who you are?
7. What have you learned—or are you now learning—because of the problems of your child?

—4—

Grace Among Others

> O strengthen me, that while I stand
> Firm on the Rock and strong in thee,
> I may stretch out a loving hand
> To wrestlers with the troubled sea.
>
> —Frances Ridley Havergal

O UR LIVES ARE NOT LIVED IN A VACUUM. As consuming as a relationship with a troubled child may be, each of us has a network of many other significant relationships, some of which we experience daily and some less often. As we hurt over a child, these other important people impact us, and we continue to impact them. The potential for strain and stress spreading to these other relationships is great. But the potential for the spreading of God's grace is greater.

NEEDING UNDERSTANDING

Parents who are struggling want and need understanding support from coparents, their other children, relatives, and friends. It is usually from these close loved ones that support is most desired. And these people, generally, want more than anything to provide such support.

But it is precisely these people who may be least able to support us while we struggle with children. In fact, quite often their involvement is the opposite of supportive. It can be downright detrimental to our well-being, injurious to our fragile emotions and spirits. When those close to us fail to provide constructive support, by inability, error, or negligence, we may feel hurt, compounding the pain we already feel.

Why can't these dear ones hear and help us when we need it most? This was a common cry from the struggling parents with whom Karen worked. Along with those few family members and close friends who really were caring and helpful, they told of those many who could not or would not help. Some did not listen enough to understand. Some—even those very close to the hurting parents, such as their own parents—said all the wrong things at the wrong time. Some family members and friends avoided the hurting parents and their children altogether during the difficult times.

Why was it so hard for others to deal with, for instance, a situation of premature birth? There could certainly be all kinds of specific reasons, but there were several general explanations that often applied:

- lack of objectivity from their close connections to the sick child and the parents
- inadequacies in understanding and communicating their own feelings
- personal fears for themselves and their children
- assumptions that a child's problems stemmed from parents' failings

We started this book discussing expectations. How very important they are in determining our responses to our circumstances. The higher our expectations, the greater potential there is for disappointment and accompanying misunderstanding.

It seems natural, logical, that we would expect our husbands and wives, our parents, our other children, our best friends, to be tremendous sources of understanding and comfort as we deal with children who are not doing well. But if we have such lofty expectations, we are very likely to be disappointed. Our loved ones may be helpful, even understanding to a point. But we cannot expect them, for a vast array of reasons, to feel just as we do or to truly understand what we are going through. Remember how intense and personal a parent's feelings and experiences are! No one else—not even the child's other parent—is going to be able to feel just as we do.

So start with realistic expectations. Assume that you will be mis-understood. Assume that others closest to you will interpret circum-stances differently and be on a different timetable from you in addressing them. Assume that people will have their own emotional issues that will prevent them from giving you the help and comfort that you most desire.

What is more, not even the most understanding person can solve your problems for you. The false expectation that someone else can rescue you is dangerous, setting you up for further disappointment.

Although this may sound like bad news, it is meant to be realis-tic and to help minimize your pain. But there is good news. While people closest to you may be ill-equipped to help, you are not alone. The God of grace is with you all along the way, and there are many other parents who well know what you are experiencing.

DEALING WITH CLOSE ONES

In each of our other close relationships (with coparent, other chil-dren, relatives, and friends), there are potential difficulties associated with the problems of our child. Already, we are likely experiencing a strain in our relationship with the child over whom we are hurting. We want to avoid the compounding of problems among others. We want to protect and preserve, even to improve, our other close rela-tionships. What can be expected in those relationships, and how can we help these other people in their acceptance of the child with prob-lems and of us, the struggling parent?

The Coparent

Can't we assume that the other parent, who may or may not be our spouse, will share our pain? Surely that person, above all others, will understand what we are feeling. Well, maybe. And maybe not.

Even if we assume that the other parent is also intimately con-nected with the child, there is much room for differences in response between us and that other parent. Two people, even if they are wholly committed to a child and equally concerned, will never respond in the same manner to the problems of that child. This is a fact. Every one of us parents is different, in personality and coping skills, even if we share a child.

In addition to different parental personalities and different relationships with the child, varying emotional responses may be based on a divergent view of the problem itself:

> *Different views of the "failure":* Just how serious is the problem? Who is responsible for it?
>
> *Different views of possible solutions:* What should be done by the child to try to change things?
>
> *Different views of parental roles: What part should the parents play in the child's life, particularly regarding the problem at hand?*

Even if parents agree on the severity of the problem, its origins, possible solutions, and the responses they should make, the way that one parent personally deals with the struggle is likely to be very different from that of the other parent. No two people respond to stress and emotional pain in the same way. And parents are people. No two parents respond to disappointments over their children in the same way.

Some parents want to talk about problems nonstop. Others talk for a while and then want to be quiet. Others find it difficult to talk at all about such deep troubles. Some want to let others in on their struggles, while others want to keep things private, "in the family." Some want to seek counseling—for self, couple, or family. Others may be staunchly opposed to such a step.

The potential for parents hurting each other as they deal with their child's issues is great. For example, Jeff recalls, "Karen was hurt when I admitted that I needed a break from her ongoing discussion of the loss of our first child. What I needed at that point did not match what Karen needed." Under the best of circumstances, even in the healthiest of marriages, spouses should not depend on each other to meet all emotional needs. When both parents are hurting so deeply, they may need each other more than ever before. But it is during these times that they are probably least able to support one another.

The passing of time can help, as circumstances may lose some of their intensity. But during the stressful times, it is helpful to lean on a friend or family member who has distance from the situation and who is willing to listen. Honesty between parents is also helpful. It was good, for example, that Jeff clearly stated his needs, even though it was hard for Karen to hear them. Mutual assurance that love continues, even though communication is difficult, can help. Hugs, acknowledgments of hurt and frustration, can also help.

There may be a tendency for parents to blame one another for their children's problems. This blame may be in the form of spoken accusation or hidden resentment. Whether blatant or subtle, blame creates a wedge between parents. Even if warranted, blame is seldom helpful. For blame focuses on the past, which we cannot change. Escaping the temptation to blame will require forgiveness and a focus on the present. It will require clear communication about "where we go from here" and a willingness to examine our own responsibilities.

The rate of divorce among parents of children with a medical disability is about 80 percent. One wonders about the numbers for parents of children with significant nonmedical problems. How well do those couples weather the storms of their children's problems and the additional stress of misunderstanding, blaming, or resenting each other? Clearly, parents are confronted with a great deal when their children have problems. It is amazing, a small miracle, when parents stick together through strong family hurt.

Friedrich Nietzsche once wrote, "What does not kill me, makes me stronger." These are wise words. Parents should remember them, as dealing with the problems of their children can potentially make or break marriages. With parental feelings running deep, the chance for marital strife over troubled children is great. By the light of God's grace, parents can travel together—sometimes at different paces, though still in sight of each other—through the dark valleys of parenting. And the walk can bind a husband and wife more deeply as one.

Other Children

In considering other children in a family where one child is experiencing difficulty, Jesus' parable of the prodigal son again comes to mind. Remember that there also was an older, more dutiful son. Read Jesus' telling of the conversation between the father and this older son as the return of the prodigal is being lavishly celebrated:

"Then he became angry and refused to go in. His father came out and began to plead with him. But he answered his father, 'Listen! For all these years I have been working like a slave for you, and I have never disobeyed your command; yet you have never given me even a young goat so that I might celebrate with my friends. But when this son of yours came back, who has devoured your property with prostitutes, you killed the fatted calf for him!' Then the father said to him, 'Son, you are always with me, and all that is mine is yours. But we had to celebrate and rejoice, because this brother of yours was dead and has come to life; he was lost and has been found.'" (Luke 15:28-32)

The older brother's joy was clearly less than full. He was far too angry and confused to rejoice or to see how his father truly felt. It is easy to imagine that the younger brother had been his parents' focus all the while he was away in the far country. These parents probably waited and watched, hoping against hope that someday the rebel would return. From his perspective, the dutiful brother saw his younger brother as receiving more attention, more love, from his parents. Now this good-for-nothing brother was getting all the attention in person. His long-awaited homecoming was marked not with consternation but with an extravagant party. Blinded by his pain and frustration, the dutiful son could not imagine celebrating such a louse! Life, in his eyes, was far from fair. Where, he surely wondered, was the reward for doing the right thing all the time?

Modern siblings can also feel this way. In the world of children with special needs, for instance, the Sibling Support Project and other experts have recently recognized that other children in those families have their own particular needs as siblings of special children. Often, these children have to grow up quickly, facing difficult feelings and taking on responsibility early. One attempt to help these siblings is through workshops called Sibshops where they can interact with other siblings of children with special needs. Sibshops provide a chance for fellowship and expression of feelings with others who are likely to understand based on their similar circumstances.

Children who attend Sibshops often report feeling left out, as the child who is disabled receives much of the attention in the family. Some are jealous of their special brothers and sisters. Some even say they have wished they had a disability to get more of their parents' attention and affection. They are sometimes angry and resentful that so much of the family resources—both time and money—go to the children identified as specially needy.

These resentful feelings can also lead to feelings of guilt and shame. They wonder, for instance, how can it be right to be mad at a poor kid who can't even walk. They also report feeling that they must be perfect, must not have or voice their own problems, to minimize the family's troubles.

Similar sentiments might be shared by younger children whose older adolescent or adult siblings are not physically disabled but who are in some kind of trouble. But even other adult children can have these kinds of feelings. Where is the reward in doing the right thing all the time? Being a responsible, loving child can be taken for granted, hardly noticed, when a parent is consumed with concern for another child.

Interaction within the family can become complicated. Siblings may blame themselves in part for another sibling's problems. Or they may become frustrated in their attempts to help if rejected by the child in trouble or even the parents.

While parents may feel compelled to never give up on their children, siblings may not be as resolute. And this is particularly true when siblings have their own sets of problems with which to deal. They may pull away from their brothers or sisters in need. They may throw up their hands out of self-preservation and say, "I give up."

This response, whether stated or expressed silently as a seemingly uncaring attitude, can bring further pain to parents. Added to the disappointment over one child in trouble, is the second disappointment that a brother or sister does not seem to care enough to help. But this is just the parent's perspective. And it is always only part of the story.

While parents struggle to find ways to help the children identified as troubled, they must be aware of the feelings and needs of their other children. These siblings need permission to work things out in their own ways. They may need some space, time away from the family troubles. Henri Nouwen addresses this awareness when he writes of the prodigal son parable: "The father wants not only his younger son back, but his elder son as well. The elder son, too, needs to be found and led back into the house of joy." "Will he respond to his father's plea or remain stuck in his bitterness?" (*The Return of the Prodigal Son*).

Being superparent isn't easy. It is, in fact, impossible. The challenges of parenting are always great. To be an adequate parent to more than one child, to balance the needs of all, is a difficult ongoing obligation. Ideally, we would not take any of our children for granted. We would give each of them infinite affection and attention at all times, as much when things are well as in a crisis. Ideally.

Even when children are small, they can see that they get more of our attention when they are in trouble. In some cases, child psychologists even speculate that bad behavior is a cry for attention. Even if it is negative attention, to a child it can be better than none at all. This may continue to be true as children grow up. They still need our attention. They need our explicit, appreciative approval when they are doing the right things just as much as they need our attention when things are going badly.

Surely it can be a comfort for parents of hurting children to see their other children happy and doing well. In addition to being a source of joy and satisfaction, those children may be supportive allies in dealing with parental hurts surrounding their siblings. Even so, it is important to remember their particular needs, too. Do not expect them to respond to the problems of their brothers or sisters in the same way as you, the parent, do. Your roles and perspectives are different.

Relatives

The web of family members who may be involved in the troubles of our children is extensive. Consider your parents, the grandparents of the child who is struggling. Consider aunts, uncles, and cousins. Consider children—your grandchildren—of the failing "child." There may also be a son- or daughter-in-law who is married to the child in question.

We can imagine these relatives' possible responses to the child in trouble and to us as parents. We can trust that their responses will not be the same as ours. And while we may be needing and expecting certain kinds of support from these family members, they themselves may be overwhelmed by their own struggles with the situation.

Karen often saw this exemplified by grandparents whose infant grandchildren were in intensive care. These grandparents hurt for their children. They watched what should have been the joy of new life for their children get turned upside down by the fear of death and disability. They ached as they imagined their children's pain. They hurt for the precious babies in crisis.

At the same time, these grandparents also hurt for themselves. They loved their children and new grandchildren. Yet they were caught in the confusion between the hurt they felt for others and that they felt for themselves. They were dealing with their own lost dreams of glorious grandparenting. In many cases, they were not even able to hold their new grandchildren. Experiencing their own pain, how could they be helpful to their hurting children?

They seldom could. More often, they feebly assured their children with statements, such as, "He'll be fine; so-and-so's granddaughter started out under two pounds, and she is a heavyweight today." The grandparents wanted to be positive. They were trying to look on the bright side, to reassure their children and themselves. They thought that was to be their role. But such wishful thinking failed to acknowledge reality and the deeply troubled feelings parents were experiencing. And often whatever was said, or left unsaid, brought out all sorts of lifelong issues between the elder parents and their children.

Most of the time we can forgive those close to us who say inappropriate things. We know they mean well. But if such well-meaning but unconstructive comments persist, we may reach a breaking point, feeling as if we must go in one of two directions. We may find that we can no longer listen to the empty platitudes and the uninformed well wishes. So we either remove ourselves from the relationships in question or we confront these other family members with our true feelings.

We often confront family members in frustration and do so without tact or good timing. As difficult as it may be, it is often better to confront a relative sooner rather than later, to take his or her aside and say, "This is the way things are. This is what I need from you. To hear you repeat that prediction again and again does not help me. I wish you wouldn't say that. I wish instead that you would just listen to me sometimes without saying anything." Just being heard is what hurting parents often want. No reassurances, no judgments, no predictions. Just a listening ear. And some of our family members may need that from us too.

Again, we come back to expectations. We may expect to receive exactly the kind of help, emotional and practical, that we need, particularly if we are new to family crises. But most of those close to us do not know how to give us what we need. Sometimes this is because of the very closeness we share with them. Keeping our expectations of them realistic will leave us with a smaller pile of disappointments in the midst of our struggles.

Friends

Friends can respond similarly to relatives. Too much advice. Too many platitudes. Not enough listening. But sometimes it is easier to be direct with friends than with relatives. Friendships often allow an emotional distance that allows for greater honesty. During challenging times with our children, this may cause us to reach out to friends more than ever. And often they will be there to meet our needs.

More easily than relatives, however, friends can choose whether they are going to stand by us during our struggles. Some, the fair-weather type, may withdraw from us. The situation with our children and our pain may be more than they can take. This happens sometimes with parents whose young children are physically sick. As parents of struggling children, we might understand that it is emotionally difficult for the family of a sick baby to spend time with families whose children are healthy. But it can just as easily work the other way around. The healthy family feels uncomfortable around the sick family. They do not know what to do or say. They worry about appearing too happy. They get tired of hearing the other family's troubles. They want the sick family to move on, to cope. They act almost as if they believe they can catch what the sick family has.

We can walk away from friends who offend us, who disappoint us when we need them, more easily than we can disassociate ourselves from relatives. But we should not do so at the first signs that our friends might be uncomfortable. Just as we are frail and imperfect, so are our friends. It may take time for them to be available to us. Or, they may let us down. But this does not mean we should end our friendships with them.

There are also foul-weather friends, those who specialize in helping others through difficulties. We may be surprised just who comes to our aid when we struggle as parents. While those we thought would hold our hands are unable to do so, others unexpectedly offer just what we need. Some, we might learn for the first time, have traveled a similar road and may be well able to offer us a shoulder on which to cry.

EXTENDING GRACE

As disappointed as we can be with others, with their responses to our struggles, we are called to be Christ to them. We are called to understand their weaknesses. We are called to forgive their limitations and failings. We are called to offer them grace—unmerited favor—whether they have come to our aid or not.

This may sound like an unreasonable call. We are the ones who are hurting. We are the ones in pain. Why must we worry about others at a time like this? In truth, you probably need not while in the midst of crises. Karen, for example, recalls making a distinct decision not to worry about the feelings of others while we grieved the loss of our first baby. She decided to focus on herself and experience the full range of her emotions. She would deal with the feelings of others later.

So be a little selfish. It's okay and reasonable. Do not worry about offending Aunt Alice—for now. Do not worry too much if your behavior and words seem strange to your spouse. Get through the crisis, dealing with your feelings as honestly as possible. While you need not throw all tact and compassion out the window, take time to put yourself and your immediate concerns first. But when the crisis begins to subside or passes, when the acuteness of a problem fades, you need to be able to get on with the others in your life. This may call for some superhuman love, tolerance, and forgiveness.

Once again, we need to call on the grace of God. We call on God's grace to enable us to do more than we can on our own. We ask for the ability to love and forgive with divine power.

Others around us are hurting for us and for our children. Perhaps their pain is not as personal or as deep as ours. But they do care, even if they are unable to clearly or consistently express that caring. By reaching out to them, you can offer God's grace—to ease their pain, to build a bridge on which you can meet, to demonstrate for them unconditional love. Reaching out requires a new vulnerability on our part. And this vulnerability can be difficult and frightening.

It is said in the community of parents of disabled children that it takes about twenty-five times of telling someone your child's problems before being able to do so without falling apart. It takes practice to be able to clearly express deep parental hurt without the floodgates of tears opening. Often, we do not share painful problems with others because we fear we will be emotional. We don't want to cry. We don't want to show our vulnerability. We don't want to embarrass ourselves or those around us. So we keep our parental difficulties and our feelings to ourselves. It is better not to say anything at all, right?

Wrong. At least mostly wrong. Sure, it is sometimes inappropriate to get into a heavy, sad matter. But it is definitely inappropriate to never reveal what is going on with us and our families to others.

And yet it is understandable that we keep quiet, especially about problems with children. Everyone else, it seems, is talking about his or her children's accomplishments, their successes. It is hard enough not to be able to honestly and enthusiastically participate in those conversations, much less to offer news of your child's failure.

But by allowing ourselves to become vulnerable bit by bit, we learn to share with others in appropriate and safe ways and to become comfortable doing so. As part of this process, reading and writing can help us take control of our pain and become comfortable enough to share our disappointments with others. When our baby died, there was almost no specific literature available to help us through our grief. A dear friend searched diligently and found us one book that addressed the topics of miscarriage, stillbirth, and neonatal death. That information on neonatal death was a lifesaver for us, especially for Karen. It helped Karen confirm that she was not alone in our experience. Had there been other such books at the time, she would have eagerly read them. Reading the stories of others that are similar to our own, we can escape seeming isolation, find fellowship, gain perspective, and release our tears.

Recording thoughts and emotions about our children in private journals, generally and in response to our readings, can also help us evoke and process our feelings. Putting pen to paper and admitting our children's situations, admitting our own difficulties, can open our minds, emotions, and spirits to accepting reality. Although less satisfying than sharing with another person, reading and journaling offer the privacy and safety we may initially need to explore our feelings. They can be steps toward sharing our truths with others.

Strange as it may sound, accepting and sharing our problems with others is freeing. Recall Jesus' words to his disciples, "And you will know the truth, and the truth will make you free" (John 8:32). While by truth he was referring to himself, expressing truth, our personal truth, can also be freeing.

But truth-telling, being vulnerable enough to admit our parental pain, is not only good for us. It is also good for those around us. For other struggling parents, it is certainly helpful to hear that they are not alone. What a light your admission can be, illuminating the falsity of the perfect child. Through sharing with others, you create an atmosphere of openness and understanding, of God's love. And who better to be a channel of God's love than a fellow sufferer acquainted with God's grace?

In this way, you become a wounded healer. Recall our similar description of Jesus. By suffering and dying, he became able to heal and save us. In a similar way, we who suffer the wounds of disappointment with children become agents of healing for others. Our sharing can make another feel less alone and isolated. Our sharing can help someone else start down the road to sharing their own pain, to begin healing. Sharing your parental pain is also helpful to anyone who struggles. It is a way to offer yourself to be truly known by another—spouse, child, other relative, friend, acquaintance—while implicitly inviting them to do the same.

Sharing your pain will also help you avoid contributing to an elephant-in-the-room predicament. This expression refers to a situation in which others are aware of an obvious difficulty—the death of a loved one, alcoholism, a serious medical diagnosis—yet no one mentions it, as though they think they can make the problem go away by avoiding the subject. Yet it looms large on everyone's mind, like an elephant positioned smack-dab in the middle of the room.

For a variety of reasons, few others will mention our children's problems. Few are bold enough to risk the unknowns of such painful discussion. Instead, and perhaps understandably, they leave it up to us to open that heavy door.

For our own well-being, it is good that we go ahead and crack that closed door, that we be honest, that we tell the truth about our situations. This is admittedly a gamble for hurting parents. Our doors of pain may be slammed right back in our faces. Then what? Will we be too hurt and discouraged to risk again?

For our own well-being, it is better to be honest, to tell the truth about our situations, our children, our thoughts, and our feelings. There may be tears, there may be embarrassing moments. But locking our pain away inside is worse, as there is no potential for healing it.

We have said it before. We will say it again. Misery needs company. But we need to be realistic about whose company we seek to share our misery. We may not be able to find that company in others who have not experienced our brand of struggle. We may not find it among our friends or relatives or in our own immediate families. We may need to look for it in more formal settings. While not all problems with children lend themselves to the support-group model, instigating new support groups or participating in existing groups in community or church is a good way to get our needs met, share our stories with other parents, and open doors for others to do the same.

Karen noticed an interesting phenomenon during her parent support organization's training sessions for those who volunteered to be "listeners" to other parents. The majority of the first training session was devoted to each of the dozen or so parents telling the stories of themselves and their children. You can imagine that tissues were passed out more than once during the evening. Every story, whether featuring a relatively lesser or greater trauma, a resolved or ongoing difficulty, was touching.

This sharing showed volunteers the breadth of problems parents can experience with their children. It personalized the training and built friendships among the participants. But it was also clearly therapeutic for parents to retell their stories in that setting. For those whose experiences were fresh, it was good for them to see the benefits of sharing in a safe, empathetic setting. For those whose experiences were more distant, it was helpful for them to remember just what they and their children had been through, to renew gratitude for difficulties survived, to appreciate progress made, and to receive new power for any troubles ahead.

It was also good for the others to listen, to hear of struggles both similar to their own and different. This was a healthy, constructive example of meeting misery's need for company. And it was helpful for these new volunteers to experience role reversal. For once, they were not the ones needing help or needing to be heard. This time, it was the mother or father sitting next to them. It was that person across the table. Someone needed them to listen and care. Based on their personal experience, that was something they could do. It was rather like a meeting of Alcoholics Anonymous, where people from all backgrounds and stations of life are in the same odd club because of their similar painful experiences. All are needy, but they all can also lend understanding ears.

What was most intriguing to Karen in this process was a universal response that seemed to say, "Wow! I could never handle what you've been through. That must be so difficult. How have you ever managed?" Everyone thought that about everyone else—even parents who had faced terrible times with their children, even parents who had lost a child, even parents whose children lived with potentially terminal illnesses, even parents whose children would always be disabled. They each thought that the others' lists of troubles were somehow worse than their own.

This recognition was not some form of parents denying what they were going through. Rather, it seemed to be a matter of familiarity versus unfamiliarity. Each parent knew what it was like to live their lives with their own child's particular medical struggles. But they were not familiar with the scenarios described by the other parents. As the parents got practice telling their stories to an empathetic group, every parent appeared to every other parent as strong for having endured a unique trial. And as they listened, every parent learned something new and deepened their compassion for others. This is what can happen within support groups.

You may be fortunate enough to know another hurting parent or two who can act as your own informal support group. If not, you may benefit from participating in a group that meets regularly for the purpose of listening to one another. Support groups already exist for parents of children with certain specific kinds of struggles. For instance, there is Al-Anon nationwide. This is not just for parents but for family members of alcoholics and other substance abusers. In some areas, there are support groups for family members of HIV-positive individuals. Some prisons have support groups for families of inmates.

While groups such as these each focus on a common root problem, support groups for parents may not. In fact, their focus tends to be on general parenting issues. This can make for pretty eclectic groups. Imagine: "My son dropped out of graduate school" compared with "My daughter is a drug-addicted prostitute." A vast range of potential issues could be discussed. But even within more specifically defined groups, there is a range of severity within a single issue.

There will always be differences among hurting parents. Remember that we and our children are all unique. There are similar situations, but none are ever exactly the same. What we need as parents is not necessarily someone who shares a common situation with us. What we need is someone who knows parental pain and is willing to listen to us and let us in on their pain as well. Even a loosely defined group of hurting parents can offer such an empathetic environment.

Family, friends, the church, and professional counselors are possible options for support. Along with these sources, consider a group of parents. By participating in such a group, you will likely take some of the pressure off those closest to you. Parents' groups can meet many of your emotional needs that those close to you cannot.

At the same time, in every possible way—inwardly and outwardly—seek God's grace. It is the only antidote we know for deep parental pain. It can come in many forms, some expected and some surprising: an understanding nod, a touch, a sunset, a Bible passage, a poem. We will be more likely to find God's grace when our hearts are open to it, expecting it, needing it. Frederick Buechner says that those few who hear the good news of the Gospel are the ones who

> labor and are heavy-laden like everybody else but who, unlike everybody else, know that they labor and are heavy-laden. . . . They are the poor people, the broken people. . . . Rich or poor, successes or failures as the world counts it, they are the ones

who are willing to believe in miracles because they know it will take a miracle to fill the empty place inside them where grace and peace belong with grace and peace. *(Telling the Truth)*

In every possible way give grace, too. There is not nearly enough of it in this world. As a hurting parent, you are specially prepared for this mission of mercy. Who better to help and comfort others? As Paul writes at the beginning of his second letter to the church at Corinth:

> Blessed be the God and Father of our Lord Jesus Christ, the father of mercies and the God of all consolation, who consoles us in all our affliction, so that we may be able to console those who are in any affliction with the consolation with which we ourselves are consoled by God. (2 Corinthians 1:3-4)

Knowing affliction and knowing consolation, you are qualified to be a wounded healer to those in need. So pass grace on to those in need. Create more of it. Live by the words of Jesus, God's gift of grace, who said:

> "Do not judge, and you will not be judged; do not condemn, and you will not be condemned. Forgive, and you will be forgiven; give and it will be given to you. A good measure, pressed down, shaken together, running over, will be put into your lap; for the measure you give will be the measure you get back." (Luke 6:37-38)

Give grace—unmerited favor—to your child. Give grace to your family. Give grace to other hurting parents. And trust God to provide as you go through this adventure of parenting, of life, with all its hills and valleys, with its joys and pains. And journey on with the grace of God.

CONSIDER SHARING GRACE WITH OTHERS

1. Who close to you understands your parenting situation?

2. What close relationship is most difficult for you when it comes to dealing with matters involving your child—coparent, other child, relative, friend? Why?

3. What is the worst thing that could happen if you took a chance and told someone the truth about your child? Is it worse than the pain you feel as a result of your isolation or secrecy?

4. What could you do or say in the near future to open the door of your pain to someone else?

5. What kind of parent support group would you like to participate in? Does such a group exist? Is there a need for such a group in your community? Could you help to start it?

6. Who needs your grace in dealing with you and/or your child? How can you give this gift of grace?

"My grace is sufficient for you, for power is made perfect in weakness."

—2 Corinthians 12:9

—Appendix—

How the Church Can Help Parents in Need of Grace

Rejoice with those who rejoice, weep with those who weep.

—Romans 12:15

LIKE MOST PASTORS, Jeff's ministry includes counseling with parishioners. The problems for which people seek help and guidance are many and varied. Commonly they include grief, marital concerns, and addictions. These are areas where in recent decades people have been encouraged to "talk" to professionals and peers, to get support and counseling. It is okay, even expected, to seek help for these struggles.

But, curiously, very few parents have come to Jeff over the decades of his ministry to talk about their children's problems. Yet underneath a veneer of family perfection, there seem to be plenty of hurting parents within the church. They are often the ones who silently weep during the singing of hymns, discreetly dabbing at their eyes, hoping no one will notice. Why aren't they seeking help within the church? Based on the fact that no one seems to talk much at church about troubled children or hurting parents, these kinds of assumptions may be behind their choosing to keep such pain private:

- They are unusual, alone, unique.
- Relatively, the matter is not that important.
- There is no help.
- Good Christians should not have such problems.
- Good Christians simply persevere.

The Christian church should be a place above all others where parents struggling with imperfect children can find grace-filled support and help. The church is, after all, a community of "sinners saved by grace." It is not a club for saints.

And yet some hurting parents who have dared to seek grace from the community of faith bear the scars of their vulnerability. We hear of churches that explicitly condemn and ostracize families with children who are not living up to congregational standards. More likely than such overt shunning, however, is the subtle, implied message that something must not have been spiritually right in the home if a child is not doing well. Such a message is judgmental, pious, and ignorant of suffering. It is, simply, devoid of the compassion of Jesus.

So, many parents keep up a good front within the church. They maintain their secret of a troubled child out of shame or out of fear of the stigma that may come from revealing it. Some compromise their church participation. One mother Jeff knew did not participate in communion because she did not feel worthy on account of her child's problems. Other parents run far from the church when their children are in trouble.

This ought not to be so! Clergy and laypersons are called together to create an environment of grace for all. To do this requires a greater awareness of the ways in which our churches can promote mercy rather than perfection.

MODELING GRACE, NOT PERFECTION

The idea for this book took root at a denominational conference when a new executive director was introduced to the several thousand attendees. This man, admired for his personal integrity along with pastoral and leadership skills, was well-known to the group gathered. There was every reason to believe that he lived as admirable a life behind closed doors with his family as he did in public ministry.

During his introduction, this leader's wife and children were invited to stand with him on the platform. The oldest child was accompanied by his wife and baby, and it was announced that they were becoming missionaries with the denomination. All members of the family were attractive, smiling, seemingly glad to be there, in a picture of unity. They looked perfect—not fake and overdone, but truly full of happy goodness. There they all were, it seemed, a shining example of reward for a life given to God and lived righteously, a glowing testimony of God's blessing for faithful service.

So what was wrong with the picture? Wasn't that what we all desire, what we all aim for? Yes, but that was not what many other faithful servants of Christ there that day, both clergy and laypeople, had experienced. Surely there were many watching that happy scene who had known quite the opposite with their families.

In fact, seated on either side of us were pastors whose experiences with children had been far from picture-perfect. On our right sat a pastor and his wife, both in their seventies. For decades, they had devoted their lives to family and church. Among their children, there had been out-of-wedlock pregnancies, divorces, one child never married, not to mention numerous problems with grandchildren. Not one of their children had experienced a lasting marriage. Although there was much joy in the couple's relationships with their offspring, they had known great disappointment in their children, much of which they still struggled with, wondering why and blaming themselves.

On our left was another friend, a man whose child had been divorced twice and who continued to struggle financially and emotionally. Another child had come short of parental expectations educationally and in terms of certain moral choices. This man remarked wryly that he could just picture his sick wife being rolled out onto the stage on a cot and his rebellious grandson skateboarding out in super-baggy jeans. This scene was markedly different from the one we were all viewing!

We well knew the two families represented by those sitting next to us. We were quite sure that the parents involved, though not perfect, had faithfully and lovingly raised their children. But their results were not like the apparent results of the man on stage. What message was going out to these hurting parents in those moments? What did they feel? It was probably something like this: If we had been as good, as righteous, as godly, as devoted, our families would look and be perfect too.

Is this the message that our churches should be sending? Is it perfection that we want to model? We think not. For Christians are not called to display our perfection but our vulnerable need for grace and forgiveness.

The most potent determinant of a congregation focusing on grace is leadership that models giving and receiving grace. This comes down to clergy and lay leaders who are real, who are genuine, who demonstrate an integrity between the personae they display to the congregation and the people they *really* are. While it is true that none of us behaves "in public" precisely the way we do behind closed doors at home (yes, we yell at our kids sometimes, and yes, we say bad words at home once in a while, and no, we would not act that way in public), the disparity between what we show others and what we hide should not be too great. And, even when we are on our best public behavior, we need not pretend that we are perfect.

In two decades of ministry, dozens of parishioners have remarked in amazement at how real Jeff is. And what else should a pastor be? Yes, a pastor is, presumably, called by God to his or her work. (We hope that we all are, clergy or not.) But a pastor is, after all, a mere mortal. Those who have remarked gratefully on Jeff's "realness" have obviously never experienced that before in a pastor. How sad. But instead of being let down by a pastor who is a regular guy, a regular person like them, they are encouraged to know a minister who they feel is human, on their level.

And isn't that what we all need to be to each other in the church? Not pretend saints, parading our skin-deep holiness in front of others. Rather, we need to be who we really are. Doing so is not always pretty, but it is who Jesus loves and works in and through each day.

MONITORING OUR VALUES

Is it a good thing to highlight for the congregation the accomplishments of families and children? One weekly church newsletter we know hails the achievements of young people—winning piano competitions, playing lead roles in theatrical productions, being inducted into the National Honor Society, graduating with honors from college, and the like.

While we in the church want to rejoice with those who rejoice, we must also be careful not to leave others out, bearing in mind our equal calling to weep with those who weep. Though not wanting to put a damper on celebration, church leadership should be sensitive to congratulations for children's accomplishments. We need not stop sharing the joy, but we can become more aware of the simultaneous pain of others.

But unless we have been there ourselves, we will likely not be sensitized to the pain felt when others' joys are shared. For those of us who do know what it feels like to be inadvertently left out, or even made to feel rejected, there is a call to act as individual "includers" of those who struggle. We can also influence our congregations toward greater sensitivity. This is a way that sufferers can positively impact a faith community.

The sharing of concerns, as well as celebrations, within the church can help to develop an atmosphere of vulnerability and caring. Consider, too, such occasions as Mother's Day and Father's Day. These are difficult times for parents who receive no appreciation from their children, or who constantly worry about their children, or who have lost a child to death, addiction, or other circumstance. Other family-centered holidays can likewise be painful.

We must be careful in the church not to emphasize society's values over those of Jesus. When new members join our congregations and we list their big jobs and accomplishments, what does that say to the person who has faithfully held and excellently performed a less glamorous job for thirty years with one employer? What does it say to the person who just lost his or her third job in a row? Does the church value the successful person (and, relatedly, the successful child), who can afford to give generously to the church of talent and money, more than the struggler?

Parental pain in the church can surely be great. Among other possible disappointments in children is finding that they haven't much use for church or God at all. This is a distinct disappointment, yet one which those parents not so religiously inclined would not truly understand. There is a particular loneliness to this disappointment. It feels like a personal rejection of parents' most precious values and fosters possible concern for the spiritual well-being and eternal future of the child. The church can offer a place of understanding for this particular unfulfilled expectation and a potential group of partners who might commit to pray for the child for whom a parent is concerned.

Teaching Grace

One of the most effective pastors we have known ministered in California's Silicon Valley to a congregation full of movers and shakers, well-to-do people, most of whom were leaders in their fields of science and industry in that high-powered region. These parishioners were achievers, even overachievers. They were successful by professional and financial standards. What reached them from the pulpit, however, was not powerful sermons reinforcing God's blessing for faithfulness. What reached them was something altogether different.

From the pulpit, this pastor would regularly expose himself. No, not in the sense of a lewd flasher. Rather, he would expose his weaknesses, his doubts, his hurts. He would admit to his struggles and failings, as he walked with God and lived daily life. By setting a tone of personal honesty, he created an atmosphere of vulnerability. Parishioners were better able to admit their difficulties, including those with family and, particularly, with children. In this way, preaching and teaching can emphasize forgiveness rather than judgment, grace rather than blessing. For parents, we, too, can learn from this message. It tells us we can know God-in-Christ as being with us in our struggles, rather than meting out blessings for the righteous and punishment for the unrighteous.

If this attitude comes from the senior pastor, it is more likely to be accepted and professed by other ministers and lay leadership in a church as well. However, not every senior minister is able to be that open and vulnerable. Others may have to lead the way. Besides Sunday morning sermons, both clergy- and lay-led Bible studies can highlight grace in the struggle more than living the good life. With this in mind, deacons, elders, and Sunday school teachers can be trained in such a direction and even chosen for demonstrating qualities of vulnerability, openness, acceptance, and caring.

Other teaching takes place in the church counseling office. Here pastors can display a listening vulnerability while offering God's grace to parents who hurt. Pastors who want to develop their counseling styles in this direction might learn more from Jeff's book *When Faith Is Tested.*

WELCOMING AND ACCEPTING ALL CHILDREN

Sunday school teachers and others who work with children should be sensitized to caring about each child, regardless of his or her compliance and perceived perfection. The imperfect, "problem" child may in fact be in greater need of Christian love and understanding than the "easy" child. In addition to the positive effect on children, this philosophy will communicate to parents of young, difficult children that church remains a place for them and their families.

But this is easier said than done. Karen admits that as a preschool Sunday school teacher there were times when she hoped that a "difficult" child or two would stay home. How much easier her job would be if the kid who would not join the circle, who refused to do the projects, who responded only with angry grunts, would not be there, disrupting all the positive happenings with the rest of the group. And yet it is the difficult, trying ones among us, children and adults, who may most need the unconditional love and care of the church. Our doors need to be open wide to the troubled and the troubling. This is extra work for us. But it is our calling. In accepting all, we teach openness and forgiveness by example. We promote the notion that children, young or old, can be who they really are in the understanding context of Christ's church, where they will be loved unconditionally.

If teenagers come to church at all, no matter their appearance, then praise the Lord. Let's try not to be afraid of their attire or hairstyles or body piercings. Let's not reject them (or their parents). Rather, we want to welcome them as God's children, who are going through the very difficult process of growing up. We want to give these children a safe place to express themselves, to ask their questions and express their doubts. We need to be open to inviting all of God's children into our churches.

At church, particular caring adults will sometimes be better able to reach troubled youth than will their own parents. Church can provide some alternative role models and advisers to the parents with whom adolescents frequently do not get along. This can be especially true if children have had the opportunity to observe adults of integrity over the years and have felt safety and security in those relationships. Such adults may be able to continue or reclaim relationships with children in trouble, having, perhaps, a greater potential for making a positive impact than parents.

Beyond adolescence, do we welcome back our church's grown children who have been—or still are—straying from the straight and narrow? Do we shower them with grace or look askance in judgment?

We hope that participation in a grace-filled church will prevent many potential problems of children. At the same time, however, our churches must be accessible to those who hurt—both children and parents.

Specific Helps

Within the confines of confidentiality, clergy can enable struggling parents to discover each other. They can discreetly help parents make connections by introducing those who have similar concerns and who might support one another.

Beyond facilitating one-to-one relationships between hurting parents, clergy can open doors to more formal support groups. Parents may desire to meet together to share their feelings surrounding their troubled children. The groups could be generalized, with the core problem differing for each participant. Or they could be made more specific, based on age of children (adolescents or adults) or the particular problem of concern to parents (child's divorce, substance abuse, etc.).

In addition to offering community and emotional support, these groups may offer practical help for the parents and for the children involved. Ideas and skills that have aided coping and communication might be exchanged. Groups often provide access to information resources and professional services as well.

Constraints of experience and time may limit the ability of clergy to initiate such parent support groups themselves. But at the very least, clergy can be prepared to respond affirmatively to efforts by parents to create peer support groups, providing meeting places and possibly some guidance or leadership.

Other more general groups in the church may also offer help to hurting parents. These groups could include people dealing with a number of different but related concerns. For instance, a group for those who find holidays painful could help parents with their pain.

Smaller churches may not have enough of a population of willing, hurting parents to make groups feasible. In these cases, an interdenominational association of churches in a community might join together to create support groups. Some groups might be ongoing. Others might function for a set number of sessions.

Church leaders can be attuned to the needs of parents within their congregations. By watching and listening, they may recognize topics of interest to struggling parents—theological, spiritual, or practical topics—and tailor seminars and workshops (conducted by appropriate professionals or experienced parents) to address these topics. Out of such sessions, support groups or friendships based on common experience could potentially form.

The church can be a prime vehicle of God's grace for parents who hurt. Leadership, values, teaching, acceptance, and specific helps can all be channels of that grace, if clergy and laity will attune themselves to the needs of those in their midst. As Jesus told the Pharisees in answer to why he ate with tax collectors and sinners, "Those who are well have no need of a physician, but those who are sick. Go and learn what this means, 'I desire mercy, not sacrifice.' For I have come to call not the righteous but sinners" (Matthew 9:12-13). By God's grace, may we become faith communities that show loving mercy to hurting parents and others in need of healing.

Consider How
Your Church Can Offer God's Grace

1. Has your church ignored, misunderstood or otherwise wronged parents as they have struggled over their children? How? Is there a need for reconciliation?

2. What has your church done for parents or their children that has been genuinely helpful or healing?

3. What else could your church do to help its hurting parents?

4. Through your church, how could you help other hurting parents in your community?

Works Cited

Buechner, Frederick. *Telling the Truth*. San Francisco: Harper and Row, 1977.

Faber, Frederick William. "There's a Wideness in God's Mercy," #493. Service Book and Hymnal of the Lutheran Church in America. Minneapolis: Augsburg Publishing House, 1958.

Garbarino, James. *Lost Boys: Why Our Sons Turn Violent and How We Can Save Them*. New York: Free Press, 1999.

Gladden, Washington. "O Master, Let Me Walk with Thee," #537. Service Book and Hymnal of the Lutheran Church in America. Minneapolis: Augsburg Publishing House, 1958.

Goodrich, Samuel G. *Fireside Education*. London: William Smith, 1839.

Havergal, Frances Ridley. "Lord, Speak to Me, That I May Speak," #538. Service Book and Hymnal of the Lutheran Church in America. Minneapolis: Augsburg Publishing House, 1958.

Moore, Thomas, and Thomas Hastings. "Come Ye Disconsolate," #569. Service Book and Hymnal of the Lutheran Church in America. Minneapolis: Augsburg Publishing House, 1958.

Nelson NRSV Exhaustive Concordance. Nashville: Thomas Nelson Publishers, 1991.

Nietzsche, Friedrich. *Twilight of the Idols*, trans. R. J. Hollingdale. Harmondsworth: Penguin, 1968.

Nouwen, Henri J. M. *The Return of the Prodigal Son*. New York: The Continuum Publishing Company, 1995.

Partnership for a Drug Free America. Report on 1998 Partnership Attitude Tracking Survey. New York: Partnership for a Drug Free America, 1999.

Sibling Support Project, a national program including Sibshops. Children's Hospital and Medical Center, Seattle, Washington.

Zurheide, Jeffry R. *When Faith Is Tested: Pastoral Responses to Suffering and Tragic Death.* Minneapolis: Fortress Press, 1997.

Zurheide, Karen Johnson. *Learning with Molly.* Mount Pleasant, S.C.: Spectacle Lane Press, 1997.

Recommended Reading

On Deepening
a Personal Relationship with God

Richard Foster. *Celebration of Discipline: The Path to Spiritual Growth.* San Francisco: Harper San Francisco, 1988.

On God's Grace

Philip Yancey. *What's So Amazing about Grace?* Grand Rapids: Zondervan Publishing House, 1997.

Other Books by the Authors

Jeffry R. Zurheide: *When Faith Is Tested: Pastoral Responses to Suffering and Tragic Death.* Minneapolis: Fortress Press, 1997.

Karen Johnson Zurheide: *Learning with Molly.* Mount Pleasant, S.C.: Spectacle Lane Press, 1997.

Information and Support Resources

All information is subject to change. The publisher and authors do not necessarily endorse these organizations but offer them for the reader's personal research and evaluation.

ADDICTIONS

Al-Anon/Alateen
Hope and help for families and friends of alcoholics.

1-888-4AL-ANON (1-888-425-2666), toll-free information on support meetings in your area; 1-757-563-1600, for questions and literature.

Website: www.al-anon.alateen.org
E-mail: WSO@al-anon.org

Families Anonymous
Recovery and support fellowship for family members and friends concerned about a loved one's current, suspected, or past use of drugs, alcohol, or related behavior problems.

1-800-736-9805, toll-free information on support meetings in your area; also 1-310-815-8010.

Website: www.familiesanonymous.org
E-mail: famanon@familiesanonymous.org

ADOLESCENTS

Focus Adolescent Services
Resources, support, and information to help families with troubled teens. Offers state-by-state directory of helping resources.

1-877-FOCUSAS (1-877-362-8727), toll-free assistance.

Website: www.focusas.com
E-mail: help@focusas.com

"Buddy" Scott Organization
Dedicated to help and support for parents of troubled teens.

1-800-288-6333, toll-free ordering of practical book *Relief for Hurting Parents: How to Fight for the Lives of Teenagers,* which includes information on starting Parenting within Reason local support groups; 1-409-297-5700, for answers to general questions.

Website: www.buddyscott.com

HOMOSEXUALITY

Parents, Families, and Friends of Lesbians and Gays (PFLAG)
Offering support and education to lesbians, gays, and their families and friends.

1-202-457-8180.

Website: www.pflag.org

HIV/AIDS

Love and Action
Interdenominational Christian ministry offering help and hope to men, women, and children who are HIV-positive or living with AIDS, also Caring Response support groups for family and friends of those with HIV/AIDS.

1-800-940-9500, toll-free information; also 1-410-268-3442.

Website: www.loveandaction.org
E-mail: info@loveandaction.org

INCARCERATION

Family and Corrections Network
Providing ways for families of offenders to share information and experiences in an atmosphere of mutual respect.

1-804-589-3036 or 1-804-589-6520.

Website: www.fcnetwork.org
E-mail: fcn@fcnetwork.org

National Institute of Corrections Information Center

1-800-877-1461, toll-free ordering of Directory of Programs Serving Families of Adult Offenders.

E-mail: asknicic@nicic.org, to order Directory of Programs Serving Families of Adult Offenders.

MEDICAL PROBLEMS

Rest Ministries
For people who live with chronic illness or pain; also includes support for their families, friends, and caregivers.

1-888-751-REST (1-888-751-7378), toll-free information; also 1-619-237-1698.

Website: www.restministries.org
E-mail: rest@restministries.org

MENTAL ILLNESS

National Alliance for the Mentally Ill
Efforts include support to persons with serious brain disorders and to their families. Offers Family-to-Family Education Program, focusing on schizophrenia, bipolar disorder (manic depression), clinical depression, panic disorder, and obsessive-compulsive disorder (OCD).

1-800-950-NAMI (1-800-950-6264), toll-free help line; also 1-703-524-7600.

Website: www.nami.org

National Depressive and Manic Depressive Association
Educating patients and families about the nature of depressive and manic-depressive illness and fostering self-help.

1-800-826-3632, toll-free assistance; also 1-312-642-0049.

Website: www.ndmda.org, includes information on support groups and links to sites of many other helpful organizations.